CAN I RECYCLE MY GRANNY?

ABOUT THE AUTHOR

Ethan Greenhart is the satirical creation of the journalist Brendan O'Neill. 'One of this country's sharpest social commentators' (*Daily Telegraph*), O'Neill is editor of the online magazine *Spiked*, and also publishes widely, in the *Guardian*, *New Statesman*, *Spectator*, *The Sunday Times*, BBC News Online, *Salon*, *Slate*, and many more.

CAN I RECYCLE MY and 39 other eco-dilemmas GRANNY?

ETHAN GREENHART of SPIKED

HODDER

First published in Great Britain in 2008 by Hodder & Stoughton
An Hachette Livre UK company

1

Copyright © Spiked Limited 2008

The right of Spiked Limited to be identified as the
Author of the Work has been asserted by them in accordance
with the Copyright, Designs and Patents Act 1988.

A CIP catalogue record for this title is available from the British Library

ISBN 978 0340 95565 9

Typeset in Sabon by Hewer Text UK Ltd, Edinburgh
Printed and bound by Mackays of Chatham Ltd, Chatham, Kent

Hodder & Stoughton policy is to use papers that are natural, renewable
and recyclable products and made from wood grown in sustainable
forests. The logging and manufacturing processes are expected to
conform to the environmental regulations of the country of origin.

Hodder & Stoughton Ltd
338 Euston Road
London NW1 3BH

www.hodder.co.uk

I dedicate this book, in no particular hierarchical order, to Gaia, my lentil plants, my children, the insects that labour under the tyranny of mankind, Sheba, and Al Gore.

Contents

INTRODUCTION

Let me introduce myself. My name is Ethan Greenhart. I write a weekly ethical lifestyle column for the online magazine *Spiked*. Most ethical lifestylists use the term 'carbon footprint' to describe humanity's impact on the planet, and there are a host of books – or what I prefer to call a 'holocaust of books', considering the number of trees that have been pulped to produce them – offering advice on how to reduce one's 'carbon footprint'.

That phrase doesn't cut it for me. Footprints are dainty little things that we leave in the sand or the snow. I prefer to write about the 'carbon skidmark' on the planet – the long, streaky, stinking stain that we have left on Gaia's pretty face. This book will help you to calculate the length of your own skidmark, and offer you advice on how to wipe it clean. Consider its pages a sort of eco-detergent (but with no nasty toxins) with which you can make your life dazzlingly white once more.

Modern life is an ethical minefield. Every week my mailbox bulges with emails begging for advice. People ask me about the ethics of everything from having children (unethical) to eating chocolate (extremely unethical) to hosting dinner parties (ethical only if the food is locally sourced and slowly cooked; if the napkins are made from undyed, recycled sackcloth; if the wine has a label guaranteeing that 'No grapes were harmed in the production of this beverage'; and if the guests are willing to recycle the food they have eaten as 'humanure' through a process known as thermophilic decomposition).

Having been a dispenser of ethical wisdom for nearly five years now, I've come to a startling realisation: everything we do is unethical! It is unethical to start a family because the planet is already dangerously overcrowded – but it is unethical to prevent the pitter-patter of tiny carbon footprints by taking the Pill (which was tested on animals!) or wearing a condom (which is made from the milky tears wept by the rubber tree!).

It is, of course, unethical to fly or to drive a car; that goes without saying. But it is also unethical to ride a bike, since the inner tube of a bike's tyres is made from butyl, which is a petroleum derivative. A recent study suggests it is even unethical to walk . . . a three-mile journey by 'Shanks's pony' uses up 180 calories; it takes 100g of beef to replace these calories; and in producing this amount of beef, the meat-murder industry (otherwise known as 'factory farming') will emit 3.6 kg of CO_2. So, your Sunday wander through a wood is energised by nearly four kilos of CO_2 – and CO_2, sticking with the skidmark theme, is easily the most disgusting 'number two' of all. What is an ethical person to do faced with these disturbing facts? Stay still forever? Is immobility the highest form of ethical existence?

When all is said and done, it is unethical to be alive. As we walk, work, eat, play and defecate, we're continually spreading our carbon skidmark. But then, it's also un-ethical to die. If you are cremated, your vaporised fillings will emit toxic fumes into the environment, and if you are embalmed the chemicals injected into your body and spread on to your skin will harm the soil and the various creepy-crawlies that live within it. And tell me this: what gives humankind the right to deny famished maggots access to their rotting flesh by surrounding themselves with a protective embalming fluid? Even after death, our arrogance lives on.

Faced with the horrendous truth that it is unethical to be born but also unethical to expire, and that everything we do in the middle is planet-bashingly unethical too, I have developed a new way of living: a zero-carbon, no-driving, faeces-recycling lifestyle which has helped me to reduce my carbon skidmark from 218 miles a year to just 0.8 miles a year! If betting was ethical, I would wager that I have the smallest skidmark in Britain.

And if I can do it, *you* can do it, currently deluded reader. Leave behind all those fancy modern inventions like DVD players, food blenders (vegetable-torturers, more like), desk fans, iPods, fridges and life-support machines, and take to the tough-but-rewarding Ethical Path.

Unfortunately, by virtue of the fact that you are reading these words, you have failed the very first test. It is not ethical to buy a book, even this one. The content of this book, my weekly columns collected together and ex-panded, was certainly *produced* ethically: my home com-puter gets its electrical current from a treadle pump in the cellar worked by my two children. It's a win-win situation: they get exercise, and I get to exorcise my ethical demons in a weekly column. But the end product that you hold in your hands, like every other paper-published manuscript, is a horrific mish-mash of wood pulp and chemically enhanced dyes known as 'ink'.

It could have been so different. I pleaded with Hodder to publish the book on rice paper with soya ink. Then we could have included instructions for readers to eat the book after reading it – thus literally, as well as metaphorically, digesting its message – and let it pass through their systems. The resultant faeces, my pages turned to poo, could have been used to fertilise the soil that is Gaia's fragile coating. It would have been a 'toilet book' with a difference, a purely ethical text that would literally have given something back to the planet. But Hodder rejected my proposal on the health-and-safety basis that encouraging people to eat books is probably a bad idea. Bah. Some people have no *eco-cojones*.

So, reader, having already added 0.7 miles to your carbon skidmark by buying this book, you have not a moment to waste. Dig in, consume, and recycle my perfectly ethical lifestyle NOW!

Ethan Greenhart,
Kent, England,
Gaia

HOW TO CALCULATE YOUR CARBON SKIDMARK

Have you noticed that every book on green and ethical living comes with a 'carbon calculator', an idea explicitly based on man-made battery-powered technology? What message does it send to readers when supposedly ethical authors tell them that the modern world is screwing up the natural world, and then invite them to use a 'calculator', an invention of the modern world, to work out how wicked they have been? You'll find no mention of the word 'calculator' in this book. Instead, each chapter comes with its own 'carbon abacus'. At the end of every section, you will be instructed to add a certain number of beads to your carbon abacus for every eco-sin you have committed against the planet. Make a note of your bead count in the space provided (be honest!) and then turn to the conclusion to tot up your total and discover how long your skidmark is . . . and how much work you have to do to eco-bleach it out of existence.

1

ETHICAL REPRODUCTION

OK, first things first. Is it ethical to reproduce humanity? To spawn or not to spawn? That is the question – and it is one that I am asked all the time.

Every week my mailbox 'bulges' with 'letters' pleading for advice on whether it is ethical to put 'a bun in the oven'. Of course, as I pointed out to a reader recently, it is neither ethical to put a bun in the oven for real – ovens use up a great deal of gas and electricity, and buns are made with eggs, which should be anathema to all truly ethical lifers – nor to put a bun in the oven metaphorically speaking. Indeed, adding another bun to a planet that is already overrun by buns is a deeply irresponsible thing to do.

I hate to disappoint the wannabe parents who write to me, but I feel I need to tell them the ethical facts. When you 'sprog up', as some insist on calling it, you are not only creating a cute baby with fair hair and a gummy smile, you're also producing a future Scud missile of carbon use, who will strike at the very heart of Mother Earth.

From all the disposable nappies they use up in the first flush of life to the mercury pollution they will create when they die and are cremated, a new life is a new contributor of pollution to an already coughing and spluttering Gaia. People complain about second-hand smoke. Well, imagine having humanity's second-hand smog blown into your skies, trees and rivers every sodding minute of every sodding day! Mother Earth is in sore need of a 'carbon patch' to help her get over the bad habit that is humanity – she doesn't need any more habit-formers, thanks very much.

But then there's another problem: is it ethical to *prevent* the reproduction of humanity? You might think the answer is logically yes. But think about all the condoms, Pills and various other modern, resource-sucking devices that will have to be created to keep overpopulation at bay.

A condom is packed with chemicals, and the Pill, like every other medical 'miracle' (well, it's a miracle humankind has got away with it for so long), is made by torturing monkeys and dogs imprisoned without trial in laboratories. If you're serious about the ethical life, you should be seriously wary about slipping on the sheath or popping a pill.

So what is humankind to do? Fear not, this chapter reveals everything you need to know about unethical reproduction and ethical non-reproduction.

☞ Is it ethical to start a family?

Dear Ethan,
My best friend is generally a very ethical person. She cycles to work, recycles her rubbish, eats only organic fruit and veg, and she has NEVER taken a cheap flight

anywhere. Now, however, she tells me she wants to start a family with her new man! Ethan, how can I dissuade her from this clearly unethical course of action?

Suze McEntaggart, London

Dear Suze,

If there is one thing Mother Earth hates more than the sound of 4x4 wheels rumbling over her face as some big-haired Chelsea mum married to an overpaid footballer goes to collect her kids (probably called 'Kylie' and 'Dave') from school, it is the sound of the pitter-patter of tiny carbon footprints.

In the old days – the dark days before ethical lifestyle advice existed, before we knew what the long-term consequences of taking cheap flights, shopping in supermarkets and wearing Brut would be for the planet – people naively referred to new-born babies as 'bundles of joy'. 'Ah, bless his cotton socks!' they'd say. Well, Suze, it's time to face the reality: a new-born is not a bundle of joy; he is a carry-cot of carbon, a manger of mayhem, and having one is without doubt the most eco-irresponsible thing a grown man or woman could ever do.

And while we're at it, what gives any human being, new-born or not, the right to wear *cotton socks*? Aren't they aware that 'the huge amounts of chemicals needed to grow cotton seriously affect human health and the world's fragile eco-systems'? The little monsters.

Some people say that another baby is 'another mouth to feed'. True. But it is also another bottom to wipe, another body to clothe, another brain to stimulate. And doing all of these things uses up Gaia's precious resources. How do we wipe a baby's bottom these days? Well, apparently the 'old-fashioned way' – using a leaf or a washable/reuseable rag – is not to our liking, so we use toxic, perfumed baby wipes instead, which, I'd like to inform you, do NOT biodegrade. How do we clothe a baby's body? Again, our more enlightened ancestors' approach to baby fashion, where littl'uns were swaddled in the fur of animals that had first been ethically killed for their meat, is looked upon as outdated, as 'sooo 50,000 years ago'. So instead we dress them head to toe in NON-organic cotton and NON-organic denim and stick little leather sneakers on their feet even before they can walk. How do we stimulate a baby's brain? Apparently it's no longer good enough to leave them in the great outdoors to crawl among the grass, flowers and nettles, as our forebears did. No, we have to buy them electrified mobiles that sing them to sleep with mechanical voices and various other battery-powered flashy and noisy devices that will inevitably end up in a landfill where their detachable parts pose a choking risk to rats and seagulls.

So, Suze, you can inform your friend that having a baby is screamingly unethical. I know what some people will be thinking: 'But, Ethan, YOU have two children, so does that make YOU unethical?' I do love my kids, but I can honestly say that I hate having had them. And not a day passes when I don't tell them what a burden they are to the planet. The reason it is OK for me to have kids, Suze, is that I have spent virtually every waking hour of the past ten years of their existence trying to limit their carbon skidmark on the planet. And I can safely say that my children are 100 per cent Fairtrade, carbon-neutral, sustainable and recyclable.

Thanks to my and Sheba's eco-parenting skills, our kids were worrying about their carbon footprint even before they could walk. Even as babies they were eco-friendly, self-sustaining entities. For example, we didn't use disposable nappies OR reuseable nappies on our kids; instead we let them do their business wherever they pleased and used their 'output' as fertiliser in the allotment at the back of our eco-cottage in Kent. Their nutrient-rich and juicy baby poo sank into the soil and enriched our lentil plants, beetroot and turnips, and then Sheba and I harvested these vegetables to make slow-cooked organic baby food for the children. Now tell me, Suze, how many babies do you know who fertilise their own grub? In effect, our children ate, recycled and then re-ate the same meal – Lentil, Beetroot and Turnip Surprise – for the first three years of their lives!

Also, where most parents set up a 'college fund' or 'trust fund' for their children, Sheba and I have drawn up an 'eco-debt sheet' for our kids. From the minute they were born we have logged every transgression they have made against the planet, whether by using carbon-emitting products or getting into petrol-powered motorised vehicles. (Sheba thinks I went over the top with the eco-debt recording at the birth of our first child. Thirty seconds after his arrival I noticed that the nurses put a plastic tube into his mouth. I whispered to a quite exhausted Sheba, 'I'm just going to nip to the waiting room and get the eco-debt sheet so that I can record his contact with a probably non-sustainable form of plastic.' 'Give it a rest for God's sake!' she shouted, though I'm sure it was just the epidural – which she took AGAINST my better ethical advice – talking.) Where 'college funds' are designed to assist children when they leave home, our eco-debt sheet forbids either of our children from leaving home UNTIL they have offset all the carbon they may have accidentally or purposely emitted in the first flush of life. Our older kid, who loves surfing despite my warnings to him that surfboards are made from a nasty cocktail of synthetics and glass fibres that might potentially harm sea beasts, has a lot of work to do if he has a hope in man-made hell of leaving home when he reaches eighteen.

Suze, I have neutralised my children's existences – and unless your friend is willing to do the same with her future kids, then she is committing an unethical crime of the highest order by sprogging up.

Is it ethical to adopt an African child?

Dear Ethan,
As a fully eco-aware woman, I have no intention of giving birth. I know very well that there is nothing worse for the planet than creating another resource-nipper. So I am considering adopting a child from Africa instead. I figure that if Madonna can do it, so can I – plus I will be RECYCLING a baby rather than creating a new life. I have been sponsoring an African

girl for the past six years, and wonder if I should now adopt her. I'm sure her parents wouldn't mind. What do you think, Ethan?

Poppy Makepeace, London

Dear Poppy,

Just the other day, Sheba and I hosted a lentil loaf get-together in our eco-cottage (lentils, organic and grown with humanure; loaf cooked in a slow-heating stone slab oven rather than by gas or electricity), when there was an almighty bust-up. Margo and Zac, who have adopted two beautiful Chinese children, clashed with Emine and Rafe, who think that transporting children from the developing world is unethical.

Why? Because a) it involves *flying* children thousands of miles around the globe (apparently transporting them in the cargo holds of freight ships is not a good idea, or at least that's what the adoption agency told Margo and Zac when they asked if Zi and Lei could be brought to Britain in such an eco-friendly fashion); b) the children will become bigger emitters of carbon – or 'toxic toddlers', as Emine rather unthinkingly called them – in our fake-tanned, consumption-crazed, plastic-wrapped society than they ever would have in their more humble, and thus more ethical, homelands; and c) the children will live for longer thanks to the West's 'miracle' of modern medicine (miracle?! tell that to the monkeys imprisoned in torture labs) and as a result will plod their carbon footprint on Gaia's face for about thirty years more than their peers in their land of origin.

Boy, did things get heated! Voices were raised in anger. Unbleached natural brown napkins made from recycled sackcloth were thrown down in frustration. And Margo and Zac left BEFORE the cheese-and-biscuits course – which would have been highly unusual behaviour at the best of times, never mind on a night when we served Taleggio cheese (we *occasionally* treat ourselves to dairy products) and crackers made with Fairtrade, rainforest-friendly, Soil Association-approved ingredients by disadvantaged youth in a young offenders' institution in Kent. I haven't seen such heated antics at a dinner party since I lost the plot at Rafe's in 2006, after discovering that the beetroot in his beetroot-and-turnip flan was not organic.

Emine and Rafe were being a little unfair. Margo and Zac *have* taken precautions to ensure that Zi and Lei leave the same-sized carbon footprint in Britain as they would have done in China. They are great believers in preserving the children's cultural heritage rather than turning them into 'little Brits'. So they have installed a paddy field in their back garden in Gillingham where the children spend between six and eight hours a day at work on rice crops; this is their staple food, just as it would have been if they had stayed in that orphanage in Xinjang. The children are not allowed to vote at family meetings because Margo and Zac feel it is unfair to introduce them to the alien Western concept of democracy. And they are forbidden from using Google and certain other websites: a rule which both respects their Chinese roots *and* helps Margo and Zac save on electricity use.

However, Poppy, despite the loveliness of Margo and Zac's kids – and the tonnes of lovely rice they have harvested for our eco-dinner parties in recent years – I must say I side with Emine and Rafe on this issue. It is definitely eco-irresponsible to uproot children who live supremely ethical lives in the Third World – where they build their own homes from mud, grow their own food from scratch, and draw their own water from wells – and bring them to a country where everyone insists on living in concrete houses, buying their food in supermarkets (eeeurgh), and getting their water from taps. Yes you would be recycling a Brownfield baby (so to speak!) rather than creating a new Greenfield life, but you would also be disturbing Gaia's ethical balance.

Consider Madonna and her adopted baby David from Malawi. Using my carbon abacus (made from sustainable wood and brazil nuts) I've worked out that Madonna's flights to and from Malawi, the car journeys from Heathrow airport to her home, the paparazzi's use of digital cameras to snap adoptive mother and child, and the rainforest's worth of paper used by the media to tell David's story have all contributed to the emission of 11,436.222222 (recurring) tonnes of carbon – which is about the same amount produced by 100,000 African children in a year! In short, Poppy, Madonna has increased by 100,000 the amount of carbon getting in Gaia's eyes. Pop goes the planet.

Poppy, if you're still really determined to adopt from Africa, then make sure your adopted child lives a carbon-lite, sustainable and culturally appropriate existence. Take a leaf from my and Sheba's (recycled) book. Like you, we used to sponsor a child in Africa.

Her name was Chloe. Well, we called her Chloe. Her birth name – Abeiuwa Bombata Obakhavbaye – would not fit on the non-chemical-based plastic wristbands we had made to raise awareness about our kindness in sponsoring a poverty-stricken African. We sent Chloe £5 a month, which helped to sustain both her and her donkey. Some of the money was spent on schoolbooks made from recycled paper, non-lead-based pencils and a uniform made from organic cotton, so that Chloe could finish her secondary education in an ethical fashion. Every year we were sent a photo of her grinning like a sunbeam at the front of her classroom! In 2005, we brought Chloe over to Kent for a two-week visit, but we were adamant that she would not feel like a fish out of water, and more importantly that she would not emit over and above her usual quota of CO_2 while she was here. So we built a mud hut for her in our back garden. We hid all our children's sustainable-wood toys so that she would not be tempted by Western luxury. We provided her with scythes and hoes so that she could harvest lentils from our allotment in a sustainable, NGO-approved fashion, and only allowed her to cook her meals and eat outside. She defecated in a nearby river rather than into our thermophilic compost toilet. When she said to me, 'I never knew England was so similar to Africa . . . I was expecting more bright lights and fun,' I knew I had successfully prevented her from becoming culturally disorientated during her visit.

Poppy, are you ready to make a mini-Africa for *your* African child? If not, then please leave those kids to their

Gaia-friendly, eco-equilibrated, mud-cherishing lives on the glorious green continent, and buy yourself a pup instead.

☞ **Is it ethical to use a condom?**

Dear Ethan,
I recently started Uni, where I've been seeing a
beautiful girl for the past two weeks. I think I'm
finally going to get lucky with her soon! Of course, as
observant eco-warriors, we have no desire whatsoever
to start a family, and my lady friend does not take the
Pill because of its origins in animal testing. So, this is
just a quick note to check with you that it's OK for
me to use a condom. Cheers, dude.

Paulie Wren, Oxford

Dear Paulie,
Yes, you may use a condom on Saturday night, as you make sweet love to your girlfriend and lose yourself in orgasmic pleasure. Alternatively, you may wish to take a stroll to your local petrol station, pump some of the black stuff into a bucket, and hurl it over nearby autumnal trees and flowers while shouting 'Global warming is a myth!' Because, my dear, deluded student, that would be on a par with the eco-crime of wrapping your penis in a piece of rubber that takes years to biodegrade as it floats from our sewage systems into the weeping blue sea.

Paulie, what are you thinking!? A condom?! Condoms are doused in a non-ionic detergent, spermicide, which contains a man-made substance called nonoxynol-9, an alkylphenol ethoxylate that is made in laboratories by attaching a hydrocarbon chain of nine carbon atoms to the phenol ring in either the *ortho*, *meta* or *para* position, and which has been shown, like all other chemicals, to have a potentially detrimental impact on nature.

Well? Not feeling so horny, now, are you? Good.

Of course, maximum respect for the fact that you and your girlfriend have taken the responsible decision to avoid starting a family. But *nul points*, Paulie, for even thinking about wearing the sinister sheath. Condoms are an affront to the natural world. For a start, they're made from latex, which comes from the sap of the Pará rubber tree, one of the most proud and beautiful members of the Euphorbiaceae family of trees. Man-unkind hacks at the body of the suffering rubber tree with a machete, then collects the milky tears it weeps and turns them into rubber johnnies to wear on his penis for PLEASURE! Can you believe such arrogance? Excuse my French, but anyone who wears a condom is literally fucking with nature. And if that wasn't bad enough, latex condoms also have man-made stabilisers, preservatives and vulcanising (hardening) agents, which means they are not very biodegradable. Your flushed-away condom ends up as a disgusting blemish on coral reefs or the sea grasses. We destroy trees to make condoms, and pollute the seas when we throw them away. All for three to eight minutes of sticky pleasure.

Of course, it is better not to use contraception at all. Why not have some safe and fun, non-penetrative 'eco-freaky' sex instead? Passionate kissing is a very carbon-lite form of human contact. Or you might try blindfolding one another and fondling your bodies in the dark . . . (just make sure the blindfold is not made from silk or any other breed of worm-boiling, planet-abusing material).

Sheba and I tried tantric sex once. I figured that sexual pleasure based on the principle that the universe we experience is nothing more than a concrete manifestation of the divine energy of a Godhead, and which seeks ritually to appropriate and channel that energy within the human microcosm in creative and emancipatory ways, has got to be eco-friendly, right? Yet twelve-and-a-half hours into our tantric session Sheba shouted, 'Oh, for God's sake, where's my vibrator?!!' and that was the end of that. I have told her so often that vibrators are eco-unfriendly, but does she listen? No. So to teach her a little lesson, I left a copy of the *Ecologist* on her pillow on the night of our failed tantric encounter. It contained a most informative article arguing that, 'from a purely ecological standpoint, many vibrators and other sex toys don't pass muster. They can be made of PVC and contain phthalates . . . The lubricants necessary for the use of many sex toys can contain synthetic substances derived from petrochemicals and are likewise unsound.' I hope that opened her eyes to the eco-crime that is unethical self-pleasure.

I know what people will say about my anti-condom stance – that I am promoting unsafe sex and the spread of disease. Well, now might be a good time to quote those brave souls in Earth First!, a campaign group I much admire, who said in the early 1990s: 'If radical environmentalists were to invent a disease to bring human population back to sanity, it would probably be something like AIDS . . . the possible benefits of this to the environment are staggering . . . just as the Plague contributed to the demise of feudalism, AIDS has the potential to end industrialism.' Now, I'm not saying I agree with that statement, Paulie . . . but it's quite interesting, don't you think? I would like to throw a hopefully non-loaded, non-judgemental question into this debate: might humankind's use of condoms be foiling Mother Nature's desperate-but-understandable attempts to correct over-population through disease . . . ?

Paulie, the lesson of the day is that man's penis and testicles are dangerous weapons. Not only do they start wars (every conflict is ultimately driven by testosterone, and of course the lust for oil) – they also create new carbon-producing human life. Unprotected, our penises contribute to overpopulation; but protected by latex, they contribute to environmental destruction. Sigmund Freud once suggested that women suffer from penis envy, but every sensible eco-feminist I know feels 'penis pity'. How awful for us men to be cursed with such a potentially destructive tool! So, be careful what you do with it, and what you put *on it*. And remember that the best form of 'safe sex', which is actually safe for the planet, too, is to have no sex at all. Eco-celibacy has a lot going for it, however much Sheba might complain.

☞ Is it ethical to wear sanitary towels?

Dear Ethan,
Every month when I get my period, I get pains in my
back – and in my heart! Nature gives me no choice but
to use sanitary towels, products which are very bad
indeed for the environment. Recently I read that we
can now recycle sanitary towels. Is this true, Ethan?
Please advise!

Annabel Shorley-Asquith, Cheshire

Dear Annabel,
I know how you feel. I got my first period ten years ago
when I set up home with Sheba. Not three months after
we moved in together I started experiencing 'empathy
periods'. Every month when Sheba got 'the curse', I too
would experience backache, cramps, tiredness and other
symptoms of PMT.

OK, I didn't literally bleed. But I did bleed from my heart
in solidarity with my wife's natural and beautiful pangs of
pain. Every month, nature graciously reminded both of
us, as we pottered around in our first little cottage in Kent,
that we are animals at root – grunting, aching, bleeding
animals – and that we are as driven by cycles and hormones
and eggs as other beasts with which we share this planet.

Monthly periods contain an important lesson for all of
us. Heavy menstruation can prevent women (and their
empathetically pained husbands – sometimes my solidarity periods are REALLY heavy) from travelling, socialising or going to work. Can't humankind take Gaia's hints?

What are periods if not nature's way of reminding us that we are animalistic, and stopping us from further harming our surroundings by enforcing through blood and pain our natural limitations? What are periods if not a sign, to both women AND ethically attuned men, that we are controlled by natural cycles as surely as the tides are tugged to and fro by the moon and winds? Periods are a red line that says, 'Humans, STOP!' But do we listen? Do we CO_2-made hell.

However, Annabel, as well as being a blessing, in that it reminds us of our animalism, menstruation is also a curse. Why? Because of how WE have decided to deal with it. Just as we have industrialised agriculture, farming, travel, sex and pretty much every other area of life, so we have industrialised our response to the menstrual cycle, too. Billions of sanitary towels and tampons are churned out every year, causing the felling of trees and carbon emissions during their production and further harm to the environment in their long, lingering deaths on one of the world's already full-up landfills.

Did you know that the average woman uses around 10,000 towels or tampons in her lifetime?! According to one study of the impact of human reproduction on the environment, in Britain each menstruating woman uses between 286 and 358 towels or tampons per year, and 98 per cent of these – read that again: 98 PER CENT!! – are flushed down the toilet. A majority of these flushed towels and tampons (52 per cent of them) are released untreated into the sea. There, tampons take six months to biodegrade, and towels take even longer.

It gets worse: the plastic liners on sanitary towels do not biodegrade at all, meaning they remain forever in the sea as a pollutant and threat to fish and crabs and seaweed. It's enough to make you weep, isn't it Annabel, to think that humankind is so vile that it has managed to turn the most natural element of our existence – the menstrual cycle – into another hand grenade to be thrown at Mother Nature? She blessed us with a monthly bloody reminder of our origins and status and we thanked her by vomiting paper and plastic into her beautiful, bounteous oceans. This is a product of what I call 'aquaism', a hatred for the sea world. This abhorrent prejudice against innocent water takes its place next to speciesism (hatred for non-humans), ozoneophobia (a fear and loathing for the protective ozone layer) and mosquitophobia (the mass murder of mosquitoes by chemicals) as one of the most destructive elements of human hate.

Annabel, you're right, you do have a choice: you can use REUSEABLE sanitary towels. These are available from various eco-outlets. You simply put them on, stop the bloodflow, wash, rinse and repeat. You can use the same towels for years! There are also eco-friendly 'sea sponge' tampons. As the name suggests, these are made from sea sponges and they are very absorbent and fully reuseable. I am a little uncomfortable with the idea that we have the right to kidnap sponges from the oceans and make them into our sanitary slaves – but it has to be better than churning out plastic-lined, landfill-clogging tampons and towels, right? My favourite eco-friendly form of blood collection – though Sheba flat out refuses to use them – are

Mooncups, small soft rubber cups that collect your blood and which you simply empty whenever you need to. Sometimes I carry one of these around with me when I'm having an empathy period, just to let the forces of nature know that this is what I would wear if I literally, as well as emotionally, bled on a monthly basis.

I have finally coaxed Sheba into using reuseable sanitary towels on the basis that I, rather than she, wash 'the dirty things', as she insists on calling them! Fine, I said: there is something about washing away our blood that makes one feel in touch with nature, responsible for one's emissions, part of a natural cycle of creation, excretion and cleansing. I find the process of washing away Sheba's menstrual blood to be profoundly spiritually and ethically uplifting. In fact, I make a ceremony out of it: every month I take Sheba's stained towels and lay them in a circle in our garden; I stand in the middle of the circle and give thanks to Gaia for her monthly visitation to both Sheba and I. Then I get down on my knees and scrub the towels clean using a little warm water and soap made from elder-flowers and the sap of a tree that died naturally. Sheba says the neighbours will think I am stone mad. I've told her not to be jealous just because I am more in touch with my femininity than she is with hers.

☞ Is it ethical to celebrate Valentine's Day?

Dear Ethan,
It's that time of year again, when the birds twitter in the trees, the chocolates in pink, heart-shaped boxes fly

*off the shelves, and lovers stare longingly into each
other's eyes over a glass of champers. I want to
celebrate Valentine's Day with my Civil Partner John,
but I want to do it in an eco-friendly fashion. Any
advice?*

Paul Mayfield, Bournemouth

Dear Paul,
First of all, let me congratulate you on being a homosexual. I often wish that I was a friend of Gertrude instead
of being cursed by Gaia with the burden of swaggering,
tobacco-chewing, baby-making, foulmouthed heterosexu-
ality. (Not that I'm like that, you understand. But if you
have ever unwisely ventured from the gay quarters of
town into the straight ghettos – Bermondsey, for example,
or the whole of eco-unfriendly Essex – you will know that
most straights are.)

As every half-decent eco-columnist is aware, 'being gay
is arguably more moral than being straight'. You queers –
I'm sure you won't mind me using that empowering word!
– have mastered the art of sex without consequences,
whereas every time a man lies with a woman he runs the
risk of creating what one eco-feminist correctly calls a
'screaming shit machine': another screeching greedy toddler to be adorned in the latest Burberry jumpsuit and
Christian Dior bib.

So, well done you for being born with the most advanced human gene there is: homosexuality. I am convinced – and so is my good friend Professor Judith Wells
(formerly Professor Jude Wells), a lecturer in Environ-

mental History and Consciousness at the University of South-West-West Middlesex – that the gay gene evolved as a desperate attempt by Gaia to remedy the horrors of industrial terrorism and its ugly, demented cousin, over-population. How else do we explain the fact that brave gays smashed out of the collective closet in the late 1960s, with the Stonewall Riots in the US, and delivered a stiletto-heeled kick in the *cojones* of our patriarchal, muscular, rapacious, overpopulated, polluting society? Yep, just as Gaia reached her tipping point, their gay genes kicked in, and like a well-coiffed band of brothers, sisters and non-gender specific siblings they began fighting back against the tyranny of hetero-reproduction.

Having said that, Paul, I don't care HOW planet-friendly you and your civil partner are – if you celebrate Valentine's Day you will be no better than the suede-headed straight thugs on council estates who buy a bunch of roses for a fiver from some cockney on the side of a smoggy motorway and then hand them like unthinking slaves to capitalist desire to their ponytailed 'birds' (prob-ably called Chelsea or Britney) before having intercourse with them on a dirty bed surrounded by empty cans of 'Nelson Mandela' (Stella).

Paul, Valentine's Day is a CRIME against the planet, a capitalist conspiracy to dupe the masses into thinking that 'love' justifies everything – including £50 lovey-dovey meals in a restaurant that serves up the bloodied hides of murdered cows or the torn-out stomachs of choked-to-death geese and calls it *haute cuisine*. You and your civil partner should know better than to take part in this annual ST VALENTINE'S DAY MASSACRE of the planet.

I'm going to give it to you straight (no pun intended): St Valentine's Day is the worst day in Gaia's calendar. (Not that Gaia lives by the human-centric Roman calendar, of course; she knows full well that the moon, wind and tides, which control us humans and our menstrual cycles and personality traits far more than we know, are the real timekeepers of this ball we have arrogantly labelled 'Earth'.) 'VD' – as we might fittingly call it – is a blatant, naked, narcissistic celebration of 'human love' which more often than not results nine months later in the production of *more* screaming shit machines.

VD involves giving wasteful cards – all that paper, glitter, ink, the disgracefully animal-phobic illustrations of rabbits, chipmunks, unicorns – to people just so you can say 'I lurve you!' I learned very early on what a monumental planetary waste of paper a VD card is. At school, I left one in the locker of a certain young woman whose name I shall keep secret in order to spare her blushes. I wrote with bright yellow highlighter ink: 'BE MY VALENTINE . . . meet me on the school allotment tonight between the turnips and the beetroot.' She never showed. I learned two important lessons that night, Paul: 1) VD cards are pointless; 2) allotments are good places in which to cry, wail and unleash your angst.

VD also involves the committing of numerous 'chocolate crimes'. Do you know, Paul, that some people –

including a very good friend of mine (well, he's not my friend any more) – insist on buying 'special chocolates' flown in from BELGIUM! I'll tell you what is 'special' about Belgian chocolates: their transportation BY AERO-PLANE over hundreds of miles leaves a 'specially' enormous skidmark in the weeping blue sky. I don't see the point of Belgium. We saved them from demented German armies – TWICE – and they repay us by flying CO_2-centred chocs and apple-flavoured beer to poncy shops and restaurants frequented by eco-unaware lovers and losers. Brussels: *nul points*.

Even worse, Paul, some people celebrate VD by taking trips abroad! They go to Paris by train (travelling through that monstrous tunnel under the English Channel which has been causing massive outbreaks of PTSD – Post-Tunnel Stress Disorder – among cod, octopus and dolphin communities) or they fly to Rome or Prague and spend £500 on eating, drinking and securing a hotel bed for their annual 'special' fornication. The cost of their super-shag to the planet is phenomenal. What is wrong with staying at home, I ask you? With celebrating VD in one's garden, or at a local park (first report any shifty-looking youth to the police), or floating on a river in a handmade coracle constructed from renewable wood sources?

Paul, take a tip from me and Sheba. Every year we purposefully and dignifiedly resist the lure of the corporate and sex-fuelled monstrosity that is VD by actually taking a break from one another! I stay in the garden for a twenty-four-hour period and show my love for my lentil plants and Mother Earth in general, while Sheba spends the day with her good friend Eamon, with whom she talks about eco-politics into the early hours before sleeping on his couch. Both of us feel refreshed the next day, me with satisfyingly muddy hands and a cold chill, and Sheba with a red glow on her cheeks and a spring in her step. That's how to do VD.

CARBON ABACUS

If you have a child, add ten beads. If you have two children, add twenty beads. If you have three children, add thirty beads. If you have four or more children, where have you found time to read a book? Add 100 beads and please try to control your fecundity.

If you have ever worn a condom, add ten beads. If you are on the Pill, add ten beads. If you have ever used a vibrator *not* endorsed by the *Ecologist*, add twenty beads.

If you use tampons, add ten beads. If you wear sanitary towels, add ten beads. If you ever worked through a heavy or painful period instead of taking it as a sign to stop and slow down, add fifty beads – extra punishment for defying nature.

If you have ever celebrated VD Day, add ten beads. If you celebrated VD Day with your homosexual lover rather than with potentially baby-producing heterosexual partner, take away five of those beads. If your VD Day celebrations led you to contract VD, serves you right.

If you have ever adopted from overseas, add 100 beads. If you have adopted from overseas but have always endeavoured to allow the child to engage with his or her cultural roots, by living off the land in a deep and respectful manner, you may take away eighty of those beads.

Note your bead count here:

. . . .

2

ETHICAL FAMILY LIFE

Unfortunately, some people have already reproduced, either because they didn't get a chance to read my cutting-edge warnings about overpopulation before making the Big Decision, or because they are selfish and think it is fine and dandy to have children despite all the eco-evidence to the contrary.

I receive tonnes of emails every week asking about ethical family life. And because I have almost completely neutralised my children's existences, and reduced their carbon skidmark from the national average of 28.2 miles per year to just 1.1 miles per year, I am of course well placed to answer questions on what used to be called 'the Good Life'.

The key to ethical family living is to work together as a singular, self-sufficient, self-correcting organism. If any family member strays from the ethical path, you're in trouble. That is why I spend so much time trying to keep Sheba-the-unbeliever on the ethical straight and narrow, and why I am so worried about my eldest boy's growing interest in surfing – because if one of the atoms in your ethical cell splits away, the whole thing can go atomic.

The ethical family must have ethical children: that is, they should be resource- and carbon-neutral. It should live in an ethical home, ideally one built entirely from hemp and sustainable-wood sources, like the Greenhart eco-cottage. If you can't do that, then at least make sure your home does NOT have a flushing toilet, limit yourself to using running water once a day, and ditch your gas/electric oven for a slow stone-slab cooker.

And the eco-family must calculate its carbon skidmark TOGETHER. You're not only fretting over your own skidmark any more; you have the kids' skids to worry about too! We Greenharts have a meeting every evening to run through who has emitted how much carbon over the previous twenty-four hours, and what we are going to do – as a family – to offset it. So if Sheba unthinkingly hops on a bus instead of walking, I might plant an extra lentil stalk; if my eldest boy goes surfing, his younger brother might do two hours on the electricity-generating treadle pump. This is how harmony is achieved, both within and without the family home.

Read on to discover how your family, too, can become a resource-neutral unit.

Is it ethical to get married?

Dear Ethan,
I am writing this note to you from my solar-powered
'Greenberry' in my honeymoon suite in a gorgeous
hotel in north Africa. However, I find I am having
sleepless nights – and, between you and me, even
failing to consummate my relationship with my partner
– because I'm thinking to myself: was it ethical to get

married?! Does tying the knot mean tying the planet in chains? Please advise! I will plant as many trees as it takes to make up for my nuptials.

Helen Cox, Morocco

Dear Helen,

Marriage can be a beautiful thing – IF it's done in the ethical, Greenhart style. Sheba and I tied the knot in an open-air ceremony in Dorset. She wanted to wear a traditional meringue-style starch-white dress until I reminded her that polyester, from which most wedding dresses are made, consists of petrochemicals and is non-biodegradable, and that silk dresses involve boiling alive or electrocuting silkworms in order to extract the silk from their cocoons.

In a pre-wedding heart-to-heart, I explained that I could not possibly marry a woman who implicitly endorsed worm torture – worse, who would dare to wear a garment that was spawned from such torture. A few weeks before the marriage, I said to Sheba, 'Let's go and buy a ring,' but then, to her surprise and to a certain extent disgust, I took her to the 'Guantanamo for worms' that is a silk-processing factory. I told her to breathe in. 'Smell that? That is the whiff of a million worms being burnt at the stake of silk production just so selfish women can wear clingy wedding dresses and pashminas.' I have no doubt, Helen, that if worms could make a noise that was audible to the human ear, we would have heard them screaming, too. Fortunately, the silence of the worms was enough to make Sheba compromise, or at least relent.

In the end, she wore an off-white dress constructed from natural bamboo. The off-whiteness was chosen to symbolise man's staining effect on the planet, his despoiling of Mother Earth's virgin purity. The dress was made (or should that be built?) by the marvellous men and women at a fashion house called Bamboosa, who point out that bamboo is 'nature's most sustainable resource, is grown without pesticides or chemicals and is 100 per cent biodegradable'. After the ceremony we recycled the dress by posting it – yes, by freight ship rather than aeroplane – to a panda sanctuary in western China where it was fed to a panda called Ziyi and her four cubs. What joy it was to know that the most expensive part of our day (I was rather bamboozled by Bamboosa's prices!) was consumed and recycled by an endangered species; that the garment in which Sheba expressed her love for me later became an expression of the newly-wed Greenharts' love for the planet, as it slowly but surely became panda poo and enriched the soil of western China, thus allowing MORE bamboo to grow.

'You have consummated with me, and your dress has consummated with the earth!' I told Sheba during our honeymoon in a tent in our back garden, thinking it was quite a witty observation. She wasn't laughing. The 'bloody bamboo dress' had apparently given her a rash, and when the itching became too much to bear she cut short our honeymoon and walked the ten steps back to our eco-cottage. 'The rash is just nature's way of warning us not to take her plants for granted!' I shouted after her. She didn't respond, at least not with words that I am willing to reproduce since discovering that 22 per cent of my readers are under sixteen.

On the big day itself, I of course forswore a tuxedo. Instead I wore one of those hilarious T-shirts that *looks* like a tuxedo (zany!), which both raised a smile among our friends and families and saved me from having to splash out on a wasteful three-piece suit that was probably hand-stitched by a nine-year-old in some sweatshop in the Far East and, worse, flown here by aeroplane.

At our wedding, we used sycamore seeds as confetti, because it is part of their evolutionary purpose to be thrown and to fly. Friends said they were quite moved by the act of throwing sycamore seeds, feeling honoured to do the kind of thing normally done so well by wind and rain. Sycamores make a wonderful alternative to paper confetti, which consists of bleach and artificial colourings that leach into the soil and infect it with the toxins of industrialisation. Confetti is the wedding day equivalent of acid rain. Some friends of mine *have* tried to raise awareness of this fact with their 'Confetti Clampdown Campaign', which protests outside churches and registry offices most weekends, yet still the wide-eyed brides and grooms getting hitched around the country allow people to throw handfuls of toxic pseudo-petals on to them and the earth. At an ethical wedding, you should always throw seeds or nuts instead, which will take root in the ground instead of poisoning it. (DO NOT, however, throw Brazil nuts! A friend of mine made the mistake of chucking them at Zac Goldsmith's wedding to Sheherazade Ventura-Bentley in 1999, and we ended up with a very battered and bruised bride and groom!)

Sheba and I did not have a traditional throwing of the bouquet . . . instead we had a 'composting-the-bouquet' ceremony. We deposited our grass-and-straw bouquets into a friend's compost toilet. Then I, followed by Sheba, defecated on to the bouquet and watched as it swirled with our excrement through the process of thermophilic decomposition. The resultant 'humanure' was used to fertilise my and Sheba's first joint vegetable allotment. We used the leftover humanure, which we hardened with tree sap, to carve ornaments shaped like various wild British mammals and posted them as thank-yous to our wedding guests.

But unfortunately, Helen, not everyone has a green wedding . . . they opt for white weddings instead, or what I prefer to call noxious nuptials.

And easily the WORST aspect of noxious nuptials is the honeymoon. These holidays abroad are propelled by man-made flight, which is propelling us into a future of disastrous warming or a new Ice Age (I haven't decided which side of the science I fully support yet). I see from your Greenberry request for advice that you are already on your honeymoon from hell, Helen. You must therefore, with extreme urgency, plant sixty-five trees, ten shrubberies and four rose bushes to neutralise your nuptials.

Is it ethical to have a toilet?

Dear Ethan,
I am in the process of building an eco-cottage in deep-south Wales for my family of five (apologies for having such a large family, but I do offset their existences

religiously by planting 100 trees a year). I am
wondering if I should include a toilet in my cottage –
or is such a device an intolerable waste of water? What
alternative is there?

Bill Stephenson, Cardiff

Dear Bill,

For me, nothing better sums up human hubris and arrogance than the existence of the flushing toilet. It would take between ten and twelve redwood trees to produce enough paper to list everything that is wrong with the modern toilet – or 'bog', as some people call it. If only they did urinate and defecate in bogs, natural soily settings that would actually benefit from the fertilising qualities of human excrement, rather than in a pristine white man-made 'bog' that uses up a veritable Niagara Falls worth of water every year and requires plastic bottle upon plastic bottle of bleach to keep it clean.

Recently, we visited Sheba's parents in St Ives. They flat out refused to allow me to defecate in their back garden, despite my promise to be discreet and to spread my excrement generously on their strawberry patch. So for the first time in three or four years I had to use a flushing toilet . . . and Bill, what I saw SHOCKED me. First there was the toilet paper, reams and reams of it, the very soul of tree-kind ripped out and turned into soft, pink, scented indulgences for our anuses!

Also, in Sheba's parents' loo there was something called 'Toilet Duck'. At first I shuddered and wondered: is this a *real duck* expected to clean up humankind's gallons of crap, just as we enslave donkeys to carry stuff, horses to pull things and dogs to fetch sticks and rubber balls?! The truth was only a little less bad: it was a chemical-packed bleach which is used to wash our literal skidmarks off the side of the bowl and which in the process contributes to our carbon skidmark on the planet. There was also a battalion of 'air fresheners', staring at me ominously as I tried my very best to empty my bowels in this peculiar setting. A quick glance at the ingredients revealed that these canned concoctions contained naphthalene, dichlorobenzene and various synthetic musks – all terrible toxins that Greenpeace and the World Wildlife Fund have campaigned against on the grounds that they pollute our homes (giving rise to diarrhoea and earache among children, believe it or not) as well as the natural environment outside our homes. I had to laugh, Bill (and I hardly ever laugh – see 'Is it ethical to laugh?' in the chapter on 'Ethical Entertainment'), at the fact that we insist on defecating and urinating indoors, yet stack our bathrooms with spray-canned pseudo-smells with names such as 'Fresh Meadow' and 'Lilies In Spring'! Ha ha! If you want to smell a fresh meadow, come to the Greenhart household in Kent after we have spread the family crap on to our lentil allotment, and catch a whiff of what nature really smells like: earthy, grubby, pooey, lovely.

So yes, Bill, please resist adding a toilet to your new eco-cottage. But be prepared for a barney with your beloved! If she is anything like Sheba-the-unbeliever, she may blow her top. When I built our eco-cottage in Kent, made mainly from recyclable hemp and locally sourced, frequently replenished wood products, I purposefully did NOT include a bathroom. When Sheba saw the cottage for the first time she went ape (aargh, that is a terribly speciesist turn of phrase which even I have been brainwashed into using! What is wrong with 'going ape'?). She demanded to know where she was supposed to toilet herself, wash herself, 'powder my nose'. I patiently explained why a toilet is such a terrible invention, and assured her that I had created a small stone space next to the well in the garden for weekly washing. I also said that, if she was serious about moving in with me, she needed to know that I am so aqua-aware I only wash once a week with cold water from a wooden bucket. What is wrong with our natural odours anyway, I asked. As Napoleon famously wrote to Josephine: 'Home in three days – don't wash.'

Eventually we compromised. We built an eco-extension for Sheba that contained an ultra-low-flushing toilet, a spring-water-based shower and a make-up mirror, while I and the kids continue to wash by the well and toilet ourselves in our outdoor thermophilic compost machine. This is another thing that infuriates me about 'bogs', Bill – all that human excrement GOING TO WASTE! Don't people realise how rich in beautiful bacteria is the average human stool? Never mind 'If it's yellow, let it mellow – if it's brown, flush it down.' My motto is: 'If it's brown, spread it on the ground – if it's yellow, recycle it like a good fellow.'

To this end, we Greenharts (minus the nose-powdering Sheba) only ever defecate in the thermophilic compost machine at the end of the garden. This turns our excrement into fertiliser, which we spread on our allotment. Thus what we eat and pass through our bodies contributes to the fertilisation of what we will eat in the future – how is that for being in tune with Gaia? And we recycle our urine as a variety of drinks, shakes and smoothies. Drinking urine is wonderful for one's complexion, and for Gaia's complexion, too, of course. I highly recommend my Pea & Pee Super Smoothie, otherwise known as Ethan's Green & Yellow Shake. Contact me for the recipe.

Bill, let us lead by example, and live completely toilet-free lives. Visit my anti-toilet Facebook page, titled: 'Leave The Lid Down – Forever!'

☛ Is it ethical to bottle-feed my baby?

Dear Ethan,
OK, please don't shout at me, because I very recently gave birth and I am a little stressed. One thing I'm particularly stressed about is that this breastfeeding lark is a bit trickier than I expected it to be. It turns out that all those Department of Health leaflets showing smiling mums breastfeeding their infants on the no.63 bus are quite far from the messy reality. So, I am thinking of bottle-feeding my baby. Please tell me that this is at least occasionally acceptable . . . and marginally ethical.

Marion Woodley, Aberystwyth

Dear Marion,

Sometimes I think people send me letters as some kind of sinister joke. Is it ethical to murder my mother, they ask, or is it ethical to fly to Belgium to buy my favourite brand of chocolate – as if asking such sick and disgusting questions is in some way funny. I can only presume that your letter falls into this category, because if you knew anything whatsoever about the ethical life you would know that bottle-feeding your child is THE MOST EVIL THING YOU COULD EVER DO.

Marion, I'm a proud militant lactivist, which is what we preachers of the 'breast is best' message like to call ourselves. If you breastfeed your child you are fulfilling your sacred and natural duty as an earth mother and replenishing him with all the milk of human kindness. Ah! If you bottle-feed your child you are stuffing his or her tiny gut with powder produced in a factory by a really big and probably quite evil conglomerate. Eeeurgh! So, what kind of mum do you want to be, Marion? Caring, sharing and milk-dispensing? Or wicked, wanton and bottle-wielding? It's your choice. No pressure.

I stand shoulder to shoulder with the militant lactivists who argue that bottle-feeding is a form of child abuse. Are you aware that babies who are breastfed have a lower incidence of asthma, allergies, diabetes, ear infections and colitis? What's more, they tend to be brainier, too! A study has found that breastfed children often have a 6.8-point IQ advantage over their abused – I'm sorry, *bottle-fed* – peers. A friend of mine, Mags, is shortly due to release another stunning study about the benefits of breastfeeding. She runs a Breastfeeding Cake and Coffee Emporium in Brighton, which only grants entry to bra-less women with infants attached to both breasts. It has a VERY strict door policy. Breast Bouncers at the entrance rifle through the mums' handbags and baby bags and turn away anyone found carrying bottles or tubs of formula. Mags has successfully imposed Anti-Social Behaviour Orders against two bottle-feeding mums who tried to get into the Emporium on Carrot Cake Day; they are now forbidden from coming within fifty feet of the place.

Mags has conducted a scientific study based on interviews with the mums who frequent her Emporium, and she has discovered that breastfed babies are 83 per cent more likely to become NICER PEOPLE than bottle-fed babies. They are also more likely to live in cottages than in tower blocks, to have an appreciation for Radio 4 comedy, and to study a humanities-based topic at university than a hard science, engineering course or tourism and hotel management. Her report – titled 'A Study of the Impact of Breastfeeding on Personality, Friendliness and Nutloaf Appreciation' – looks set to boost the breast-is-best argument even further.

Marion, breastfeeding is the one issue that has almost split Sheba and I asunder. We compromise on many other things: for example, I gave in to her demands for a radio despite my implacable opposition to the movement of radiowaves through the atmosphere; and she allowed me to provide a temporary home for a friend's six-month-old lynx despite her irrational fear of 'wild' cats. That is what marriage is all about. BUT there could be no compromise on breastfeeding. So when our first kid was born and I discovered that Sheba had secretly been hitting the bottle – and was even hiding bottles and tubs of formula behind the cookery books in the kitchen – it was make-or-break time.

'How can you do this to our child?!' I demanded in an unusually loud voice. She said I didn't understand how stressful it was being a full-time milk dispenser. I said I would love to breastfeed our baby, only Gaia has cursed me with two useless nipples that squirt out diddlysquat and chafe when I go jogging in my organic-cotton tracksuit. I told her she MUST exclusively breastfeed our baby for at least the first six months, and preferably the first six years, otherwise we would have to look him in the eye when he grows up and tell him the truth about why he failed his GCSEs: because mummy opted for bottle over breast. Even worse, how would we look our *friends* in the eye? I don't know if you've ever been to a gathering of ethically aware couples with kids, Marion, but I can tell you that if you don't breastfeed then you will have absolutely nothing to talk about with them.

Sheba relented. She showed me where she had hidden all the bottles, and together we melted them down and turned them into a vase for lentil stalks. She even agreed to attend a Bottlefeeders Anonymous meeting kindly arranged by Zac and Margo in their townhouse, at which she declared: 'My name is Sheba and I fed my baby from a bottle . . .' It was very cathartic. Everyone wept. One of the other mums who had been tempted into the world of bottle-feeding brought her bottles with her, and together we stamped them under our feet and used the shards of plastic to create an abstract ornament that we called 'Regret'. Sheba agreed to the twelve-step programme: step number one was admitting she had a problem, while the other eleven steps guided her back to the enlightened path of 'breast is best'. I know she stuck with exclusive breastfeeding from that moment on, because I kept finding milk-soaked bras, breastmilk pumps and 'I Love Breastmilk' nipple guards everywhere around the house! It was almost as if Sheba wanted to ASSURE me that she had transformed into a militant lactivist just like me, which shows how much she respects my way of life.

But, as I said Marion, the choice is yours. I cannot stop you from bottle-feeding your child. But I can tell you this: if you want your beautiful little baby to grow up healthy, happy, handsome, intelligent, successful, nice, friendly, eco-aware, amusing, well-off and a *Guardian* reader, then repeat after me: 'I MUST, I MUST, I MUST FEED WITH MY BUST.'

☞ Is it ethical to celebrate Christmas?

Dear Ethan,
Christmas is coming around . . . again! I always seem to end up broke, tired and chained to the kitchen sink during this silliest of seasons – but the children do so love it. I'd like to be ethical this year, but I don't want to disappoint the kids. How can I give to them without taking too much from our fragile planet?

Maureen St John Carlisle, Surrey

Dear Maureen,

Christmas?! What do you mean *Christmas*? I presume you are talking about 'Winterval', or the Winter Solstice: the time of year when humankind *used to* celebrate the seasonal shift, rebirth and nature in general, until the whole shebang was usurped by Christians/capitalists and turned into an excuse to celebrate the birth of yet another mouth to feed (Jesus Christ's) and to buy each other woolly hats, scarves, DVDs, ties and other animal or toxin-based products we don't need. No, it isn't possible to have an ethical, much less a fun, Christmas . . . but boy, is it possible to have a super-ethical and super-entertaining Winterval!

Here, Maureen, is my guide to a Wonderful Winterval (but probably not a 'White Winterval': our ceaseless warming of the planet has reached such a level that snow has become a rarity in once-sleety Britain).

☞ **Decorations**

First things first: a dead tree *does not* bring life to a room; it merely reminds us of the horrors of defor-estation. I am horrified by the number of mutilated pines I see at this time of year. Even worse are the 'fake' trees – those plastic and tinsel-based factory creations that are a libel against tree-kind. Decorating one's home with a chopped, uprooted and trimmed tree is only marginally less evil than decorating it with the severed heads of a deer or zebra, as some hunters still do.

So, instead of dead trees, green and silver tinsel, foil-wrapped chocolates and various paper-based mon-

45

strosities, why not make your own decorations, Maureen? For example, last Winterval, Sheba and I placed the broken branches from an expired oak on our mantelpiece, and squished the berries naturally discarded by a nearby cherry tree to paint pictures of wild animals on undyed recycled paper; we also placed seawashed stones in strange and unusual patterns on our natural wood floors. The effect was very haunting. It certainly scared Sheba's mother; she said it was 'like something out of *The Blair Witch Project*', which I think is a reference to a movie.

You can also involve your kids in using recycled paper to make decorations. One of the daily horrors of my life is finding junk mail on our doormat every morning. This junk is the postal equivalent of a drive-by shooting: ads for meaty pizza restaurants and wood-stacking DIY stores chucked through our letterboxes without a single thought for the number of trees that were felled to produce them or the sensitivities of the eyes that might behold them. But we Greenharts always get one over on the consumerist/catastrophist system: we collect the capitalists' junk mail and then use it to make Winterval decorations, thus recycling paper *and* subverting our culture of excessive consumption all at the same time! In an act of eco-irony that never fails to make me smile, and sometimes cry, we use the junk mail to fashion a tall, sprawling tree on the living room wall, thus returning this wretched pulped matter to its original form of existence.

Of course, do NOT put up any Christmas lights: as we know, humankind's addiction to electricity will shortly plunge the planet into eternal darkness. Instead of traditional carol singing, Sheba, I and the kids carry out door-to-door 'See The Light' protests. This involves knocking on the doors of homes that are coated in thousands of green and red bulbs and electrified Santa Clauses and singing a ditty to the home-owners about their 'carbon crimes'. (See 'Winterval Songs' below.)

☞ **A festive feast**
Don't eat turkey. Do I even need to tell you that, Maureen? Feeding an animal for months on end simply so that it will get fat and then be electrocuted, plucked, mutilated and roasted is wasteful, bloody and cruel – as I explain to my children every Winterval morning. That is how we start the day: in remembrance of the millions of turkeys that will be stabbed, sliced and eaten over the next twenty-four hours. I read to my children from the eco-story collection, *The Turkey That Had Its Breast Carved Off, and Other Modern Tales*, and we look at pictures of turkeys hanging by their legs in abattoirs. I find that this gets us in the mood to have a truly ethical Winterval, free from all kinds of cruelty.

In the name of reducing food miles, you should of course grow all your own festive grub. At Winterval, as a change from my beloved lentil loaf, we usually have herby cabbage and beetroot potato cakes made from veg grown on our own allotment and fertilised with our own excrement. The kids love these potato cakes so much that every year they insist on sharing them with the birds in our garden; they throw huge chunks out of the window for the crows and sparrows to feast on, eco-aware troopers that they are!

A real recipe for disaster at the festive dinner table is, of course, alcohol. If I had a penny for every Winterval gathering I've been to during my thirty-six years at which booze led to blazing rows, well, I'd have at least 13p. Instead of wine or beer, serve something interesting and pacifying like elderflower cordial. I also make a brilliant recycled smoothie called the Winterval Wee Shake; it is delicious when drunk fresh and warm with a dash of eggnog (made with egg substitute, not real eggs).

☞ **Winterval songs**
'Christmas carols' tend to have lyrics that wallow in religious mythology, materialist insanity, animal cruelty or celebrations of feudalism. Take 'The Twelve Days of Christmas'. On the first day – the *first* day! – we're told that the singer was given a partridge in a pear tree. Quite apart from the impracticalities of giving someone an entire pear tree, who or what gives ANYBODY the right to trade in partridges? If you add up the various gifts in that ditty, you'll see that all of the following are treated like chattels: twenty-three birds, seventeen women

and twenty-three musicians. Like so many other carols, this one is speciesist, misogynistic and consumerist.

So the children and I have rewritten Christmas carols as Winterval songs of woe. Our 'Jingle Hells' tells of the coming floods as Greenland continues to melt; 'Cook King Wenceslas' tells of the coming burning of the planet; 'Killjoy to the World' tells of the importance of sometimes forswearing fun (cheap flights, binge-drinking, football, etc) in the name of saving the planet. Contact me for rice-paper printed lyrics and sheet music.

Maureen, see what fun this season can be? If you avoid 'celebrating Christmas' and instead give your kids an educational, ethical and elderflower-juiced Winterval, you and they will be filled with Gaia's spirit.

Is it ethical to home-school my children?

Dear Ethan,
My eldest son (also called Ethan!) will soon turn five, and it will be time for school. But I am reluctant to send him to an institution at which there will be less ethically aware children running around, and thus the potential for Ethan to get bullied. Should I keep him at home? Is home-schooling ethical?

Marjorie Aimslin, Newcastle-upon-Tyne

Dear Marjorie,

Is home-schooling ethical!? It's essential. Aside from bottle-feeding them or allowing them to eat crisps, sweets, meat and non-Soil Association approved fruit and veg, sending your nipper to a redbrick building in which he will be taught such human-centric and Gaia-phobic nonsense as 'history' and 'maths' is the most abusive thing you can do to him.

A modern, mixed, bustling school – which is likely to include the sons and daughters of factory workers (how can we be sure they aren't infected with asbestos?), famous footballers and even airline pilots and other climate criminals – is no place for such super-sensitive and planet-friendly children as ours, Marjorie. I made the mistake of allowing our eldest boy to attend a nearby comp for a few months. There was ALWAYS trouble. The other kids simply did not understand my boy's reluctance to play football (he hates the idea of kicking around a pig's bladder, OK?); to take part in gym (ropes are a no-no in the Greenhart family because they frequently contain a synthetic fibre called polypropylene which is made by the CHEMICAL INDUSTRY); and to sit through a history lesson in which the teacher very strongly insinuated that the Industrial Revolution was a *good thing.*

I was so proud of my boy for walking out of that class, yet the other kids threw pens, erasers and fun-sized Mars bars at him (using the sugary sludge that their unthinking parents put inside their lunchboxes as actual weapons), and the school branded him 'disobedient'. 'Yeah, civilly disobedient', I retorted, and withdrew my boy from that den of educational vice and grotesque vandalism (you should have seen the graffiti in the toilets) faster than you could say, 'Sir, I feel unwell . . .'

Marjorie, it would take an entire Epping Forest worth of textbooks to tell you what is wrong with school education. That's one bad thing already: textbooks. It gives me and my two boys sleepless nights to think of the number of trees cut down in the prime of their lives just so children can be provided with books on Shakespeare, science and sex which they don't even bother to read, instead defacing them with obscene doodles and inane slogans like 'Woz I ere? Yes I woz.' What's wrong with the old oral tradition of passing on knowledge? With just *telling* people things, or showing them by making temporary chalk drawings on stone walls?

I have come to the conclusion that schools are factories of conformism, where children are DRUGGED UP with fatty foods and e-number packed drinks, BRAIN-WASHED to accept the poisonous idea that human knowledge is somehow superior to Gaia knowledge or dog knowledge or ant knowledge, and TRAINED through physical education to become fast-running, heavy object-throwing, competitive lunatics perfectly suited for the world of work in our capitalist/catastrophist society.

Marjorie, what I saw when I visited the educational zoo my boy attended . . . it sent shivers down my spine. This was in 2004 BCC – Before Celebrity Chef. Jamie Oliver had not yet grabbed the nation's schools by their ketchup-stained collars and forced them to replace their fat-packed school dinners with Waldorf salads and turnip smoothies. In the lunch hall, I saw densely torsoed, thick-limbed children wolfing on things called 'turkey twizzlers' – twisted, rubbery, greasy bits of meat. They washed them down with various shades of fizzy pop, giving rise to a chorus of turkey-tinged belching, and finished off with big blocks of stodgy chocolate sponge swimming in a substance I had never known existed: 'pink custard'. My poor boy was sitting on his own in the corner of the dining hall, protecting his non-plastic-based lunchbox and his lunch of egg-free crackers with lentil-and-pea paste from the bulging eyes of curious children high on chemically enhanced turkey flesh.

Later, I watched my boy take part in a sports day. It was like a scene from Hieronymus Bosch. Podgy-bodied children in ill-fitting sports gear ran across fields carrying eggs on spoons or with their legs tied together to imitate some kind of conjoined deformity. Other children hopped, skipped and leapt into sandpits, or threw spear-like objects into the distance, as if desperate to recapture the simpler and happier lifestyles of their superior ancestors, the Neanderthals. And all the while, the kids' parents – the mums in pink tracksuits and hoop earrings, the dads in paint-stained jeans – cheered and jeered for their little Britney or Zoolander to 'whoop' the other kids 'into oblivion'.

But the worst part of the school was the classroom itself. In my boy's class, there were actually TWO LIVE GUINEA PIGS in a cage. The children named them Posh and Becks and took turns feeding them. Of course they thought it was hilarious that my boy had never heard of

'Posh and Becks', and guffawed madly when he asked why two guinea pigs imprisoned without trial had been named after a word used to describe the upper classes and a brand of beer. But it was what went on *around* the falsely imprisoned guinea pigs that was really sickening, Marjorie. In schools, children are continually and relentlessly taught that humankind is rational (as if!) and that this 'rational' way of viewing the world, through numbers, pie charts, historical facts and figures etc, is superior to every other way of viewing the world. Schools are Institutionally Speciesist.

Children are indoctrinated with maths and science, two crazed subjects that treat the natural world and its phenomena as things to be measured and observed by humanity. The arrogance! They are mind-warped with history, a masculinist and super-linear description of the evolution of things from the point of view of humankind (kings, generals, rioting mobs). The narcissism! They are desensitised to the feelings of non-human beings in biology, where they cut open frogs (institutionalised amphibiaphobia) and look at cells through microscopes without taking into consideration the cells' feelings or the question of whether the cells WANT to be looked at. The insanity! And they are taught various different languages, which is perhaps the most pernicious and poisonous part of the school curriculum, since it twists children's minds into thinking that travelling overseas and conversing in French, Italian or Swahili is a good thing, despite the fact that travel farts tonnes and tonnes of CO_2 into Mother Earth's already bunged-up sinuses. The horror!

Marjorie, home-schooling is the ONLY solution to the terrors of the modern education system. Like Sheba and I, you should liberate your kids from the tyranny of turkey twizzler-fuelled bullying and government-approved speciesist indoctrination, and teach them to love nature, loathe man-unkind, and to run fast not in order to win, but for the pure pleasure of feeling Gaia's wind whistling through their hair. Or if they are being chased by feral children driven wild by the taste of processed meat.

CARBON ABACUS

If you had a Green Wedding, good for you! If you had noxious nuptials, add twenty beads. If you wore a silk dress, add 100 beads. If confetti was thrown at your wedding, add one bead for every piece of confetti: if you can't remember (I bet Mother Earth can), make an honest estimate.

If you have a flushing toilet, add 100 beads. If you have an ultra-low-flush toilet, add fifty beads. If you have ever sprayed anything named 'Daffodil Scent', 'Spring Meadow', 'Autumn Rain' or similar, add 100 beads.

If you have ever bottle-fed your baby, there is no carbon abacus big enough to calculate your wickedness.

If you have ever celebrated 'Christmas', add ten beads. If you have ever eaten turkey, add twenty beads. If you were the person responsible for carving the turkey with a shiny carving knife before eating it, add 100 beads. If you have ever been drunk during Winterval and made fun of a host's lentil loaf (you know who you are), add 700 beads.

If you send your children to public school, add five beads. If you send your children to grammar school, add ten beads. If you send your children to a bog-standard comp, add 100 beads and don't bother asking them for help with your carbon calculations.

Note your bead count here:

. . . .

3

ETHICAL WORK LIFE

'It's my job, what choice do I have?' I hear people ask that question so often, as they try to justify doing eco-horrendous things on the grounds that they are being paid for it. 'It's not my fault that I emit so much CO_2, I'm just a jobbing bus driver!' they say. Or 'Don't blame me for the imprisonment without trial of wild animals, I'm just a zoo hand!'

I'm sorry, but these excuses don't wash with me – not even on a super low-heat, non-biological setting. We have a responsibility to be ethical even in our work lives; in fact, *especially* in our work lives, which is where we interact with other people, with customers, commuters, patients and various other categories of eco-unfriendly, often under-educated human beings, so we have a responsibility to lead by example.

As you will see in this chapter, I have developed a completely carbon-zero, non-impact form of working from my eco-home. And if I can do it, so can you. Well, not if you work in a factory, I suppose, which necessarily involves travelling by bus or car to your workplace and using grotesque machinery to produce unnecessary consumer goods for the brainwashed mass of the population. Such a job could *never* be eco-friendly, so I strongly advise that you stop it at once.

Most of the letters I receive about work ask about how to make work life *more* ethical. Ethan, I'm stuck in a supposedly paperless office but in fact there's paper everywhere – what can I do? Or Ethan, the tea girl leaves the TV in the coffee room on standby and I need to find a firm but not overly patronising way of telling her to NEVER do it again – any tips? Yet this is all just thumb-twiddling while Rome burns. (Or rather while the whole planet burns; thankfully that human-centric 'civilisation' in Rome burnt up long ago.)

No, we need to find ways to overhaul workplaces so that there is NO paper, NO TVs, NO need to remind people about ethical living because it will be part of their job description to make as little carbon impact as possible or else face the sack. Only such a top-down, tough-love attitude to making the workers greener will reduce the current 4,984,862-mile carbon skidmark left by workplaces in Britain every year. (Boy, it's hard doing sums that run into the millions on a carbon abacus made from sustainable wood and Brazil nuts . . .) As a start, follow the tips in this chapter on where you should and shouldn't work if you want to be properly ethical.

☞ **Is it ethical to work in a supermarket?**

Dear Ethan,
I am seventeen years old, and a bit hard-up. I need to make some money between now and when I start university in a year's time, or else I am destined to live on a diet of Pot Noodles and tap water. So I am

thinking of taking a job in a brand new gleaming Tesco that has just opened up in my town centre. Is this ethical, Ethan?

James Collindeep, Hayes, Middlesex

Dear James,

Blast you! You have made me itch and sting all over! I have red blotches on my arms and face after reading your bloody email. Don't you know that any mention of the word 'Tesco' brings me out in a terrible rash? Don't you know that every true and righteous ethical warrior is *allergic* to Tesco – to the place itself, to its carrier bags, to the speaking of its foul five-letter name, and most importantly to the obese consumers in clingy leggings who shop there without a care for the planet, and the listless zombies in cheap starchy uniforms who work there without a care for their own mental health? 'We're just doing our jobs,' they say, in common, monotone voices. That's also what the camp guards at Auschwitz said. Have a think about that, James.

Young man, there is no more unethical place to work than in a supermarket. An oil rig comes close, but even those horrendous Gaia-drilling machines on stilts have *some* benefits: for example, they're in the middle of nowhere, which means their usually male workforce cannot go out every Saturday night, binge-drink themselves into oblivion, and stain and litter streets, alleyways and parks with urine and reconstituted kebab 'meat'. Also, oil rigs catch fire every now and then, which I'm convinced is Mother Earth's way of telling us to stop stealing her black bile and using it to energise cars, planes and other deadly contraptions. But what benefits are there to supermarkets? None whatsoever. All they do is make shopping easier, cheaper and more convenient, and in my book that makes them the most sinister institutions in modern Britain.

Prior to being diagnosed with Tescophobia – an extreme sensitivity to supermarkets that causes one to sweat, jitter and itch anywhere within a 50-metre radius of a Tesco, Morrisons, ASDA or Iceland (but not a Waitrose) – I actually ventured into one of these buildings, James. My plan was to get a job as a Tesco worker and write a book along the lines of George Orwell's *Road to Wigan Pier*. It would have been a sociological analysis of working conditions in twenty-first-century Britain, and an exploration of the extraordinary psychology of working men and women who can stack shelves with products wrapped in plastic or cardboard, chop up meat, handle dead fish, and assist and serve clearly unethical (and sometimes unspeakable) members of the 'urban classes' without experiencing any obvious signs of eco-guilt. How, I wanted to know, have Tesco workers made themselves immune to ethical concerns? Is there a brain deficiency among these workers that makes them unreceptive to the ethical outlook, or is there something in Tesco's own garish lighting and tannoy announcements that brainwashes workers and makes them the shop-floor equivalent of a Stepford wife?

The working title of my book was *My Life as a Zombie: How an ethical man toughed it out in Tesco and lived to tell the tale*. Unfortunately it was never written. Because on my very first visit to a Tesco I collapsed in a pool of my own cold sweat right in front of the store's own-brand strawberry-flavoured milk, convulsing in agony as Tesco-phobia gripped my body and my being for the first time.

James, what I saw during my brief but eye-bulging visit to that store should put you off the idea of ever working in a supermarket. Believe me, the devil is in the detail – or the devil is in the retail, rather. First, there were the workers, with their dead eyes and cadaver-like skin. Now I know what Andrew Simms was writing about in his great and profound anti-Tesco treatise *Tescopoly* (a book I could only read after smothering myself in baby lotion and swaddling my arms and face with bandages, on account of how many times it mentions the word 'Tesco', which always triggers my Tescophobic immunological response. By the way, a quick thanks to Sheba for agreeing to type the word 'Tesco' for me throughout this piece. I have found that my fingers contort and stiffen, as in early-onset arthritis, whenever I try to type that five-letter word.) In *Tescopoly*, Simms writes about Tesco workers, modern-day zombies, who 'slump from place to place . . . listless and depressed'. Tesco is a 'spiritual wasteland', he says. It's so true, James! When I was there, I thought I had stepped into a Romero-style nightmare. Shop-floor work-ers stared at me with wide eyes, dragging their leather-wrapped feet along the bleached/poisoned floor as they moved in my direction. I decided that the only way to shake off their attentions was to act like one of them, to pretend that I – ethical Ethan! – was also listless, un-ethical, deranged, Tescofied. So I hunched my back, stiffened my arms, fixed my crazed stare on other shoppers, and walked through the aisles of plastic-wrapped produce in slow motion. Unfortunately my cover was blown when one of the zombie-workers *put her hand on my shoulder* and asked in a monotone voice, 'Are you OK, sir?' I shuddered and shouted, 'Don't touch me!' before fleeing into the nightmarish perfumed and pulped-tree department that was the toilet-roll aisle. After that, they knew I was not one of them; they could sense and possibly smell my earthy ethical origins. Two 'security guards' followed me at a distance, watching my every move.

Then, James, there are the shoppers. Now, how can I describe them to you without running the risk of being accused of snobbery? Well, the women generally wear tracksuits or black leggings, and shout very loudly indeed at their children. The children, to my shock and horror, wear trainers that have FLASHING LIGHTS on them (leather *and* electricity; how foul), or HIDDEN WHEELS that allow the little monsters to whizz from the detergent aisle to the deodorant aisle at high speeds. The men have quite coarse hands and some of them wear jeans and overalls stained with paint and dust, suggesting to me that they work in the building/destruction-of-the-planet industry.

Do you get my drift, James? These are people who USED TO BE quite decent and noble. In the past, they would have shopped at fishmongers, bakers, butchers (eeurgh!), ironmongers and street markets. Yes, such shopping was time-consuming and labour-intensive, but what's wrong with that? Having to spend hours walking from one shop to another was very good, bracing exercise, and it also taught working people an important lesson: Food and household goods don't come cheap and easy! You have to put in a bit of effort to get hold of these things! Now, what has Tesco gone and done? It has put everything the ordinary family might need – from toasters to Taleggio cheese (yes, they actually sell that, James! Of course, none of the women in leggings were buying it) – under one roof! This means people no longer have to get on Shanks's pony and traipse from one shop to another to fill their larders, but instead can get every foodstuff, electrical product and even piece of reading material (mostly rubbish books about child abuse or serial killers) they could possibly desire in the space of half an hour in ONE BUILDING! This has had a seriously negative impact on the exercise levels of the urban classes, which might explain why many of the shoppers I saw during my terrifying trip to Tesco were quite podgy.

As if all of that wasn't bad enough, James, there is also Tesco's produce. How my stomach wheeled and whirled as I walked past the meat counter and spied the severed limbs of murdered chickens and the sliced hides of tortured cows! How my eyes rolled in my head as I ran screaming past the fish counter where poor, pathetic salmon and cod were laid out on icy tombs for the zombie-shoppers to pore over and purchase!

There were also products flown from OVERSEAS. It is estimated that Tesco is the worst food-miles sinner in the UK. Did you know that Tesco sells something called the goji berry, which it describes as one of the Himalayas' 'best-kept secrets'? These wrinkly red berries are plucked from plants high up in the Indian/Tibetan mountain range, stuck in glass jars, and flown thousands of miles to a Tesco in Bermondsey or Essex. First, James, why couldn't we *leave* the berries as the Himalayas' best-kept secret instead of polluting the sky with smog by air-freighting them to Britain? Second, what's the point in selling something so exotic in TESCO where most shoppers think mushy peas is a daring delicacy?! If the goji berries were on sale in Waitrose, say, where they might be purchased by ethically minded shoppers whose children DO NOT wear trainers with flashing lights and who would probably offset the goji berries' carbon miles by planting a willow tree in their garden, I could understand it. But in TESCO?! That's just blowing a big fat raspberry at the environment.

Finally, James, where do Tesco shoppers put all their purchases? Into PLASTIC carrier bags! Britons use around ten billion carrier bags a year, and lots of them come from Tesco; each carrier bag weighs eight grams; which adds up to 80,000 tonnes of plastic being dumped in landfills on an annual basis just so that feckless shoppers can carry home their toilet paper (pulped trees), detergent (for their CO_2-emitting washing machines), deodorant (destroys the ozone layer), strawberry-flavoured milk (words fail me) and goji berries (ha ha). James, could you really bring yourself to work in a store that employs zombies, is patronised by the unethical masses, and which sells polluted and polluting products that are transported in carrier bags? Money earned in such an institution really would be the wages of sin. James, you'd be better off starving your way through Uni rather than living off the spoils of a Saturday supermarket job.

If you MUST work in a supermarket, then use your brain, James: the most ethical supermarket to work in is Waitrose because its patrons are generally nice, green-leaning people who appreciate bumpy, muddy organic produce and ethically sourced goat's milk. The worst supermarket to work in (even worse than Tesco!) is Iceland because its uneducated patrons think it is wonderful to buy frozen dead fish and animals transformed into party snacks just because Kerry Katona said in a TV advert that they were 'DEEE-LISH-OUS'. But I would advise you to steer clear of all supermarkets, James, unless you are protesting against them. Why not join me and other ethically sensitive individuals who get a 'shudder down our spines' at the mention of the word 'Tesco' as we write to our MPs, stage anti-supermarket stunts and hector zombified shoppers in our effort to halt the Tescofication of the nation? Contact me for more info about our campaign group, Tescophobics United against Tesco (TUT).

☞ Is it ethical to employ children?

Dear Ethan,
I run a carbon-offsetting company. CO_2 users in the UK offset their carbon emissions by giving us money, which we use to fund eco-friendly forms of development in the Third World. In short, caring Brits offset their toxic existences by funding a less toxic way

of life in Africa and Asia. However, I recently
discovered that some of the eco-friendly schemes in the
Third World supported by my company employ
CHILDREN! I have heard that kids as young as six are
working on our eco-friendly farms. Ethan, is this OK?
Please say yes!

Anonymous, Cambridge

Dear Anonymous,

It is deeply, deeply unethical to employ children. In
Britain. In the Third World, however, where the tradi-
tions and customs are quite different to our own, it is
absolutely fine. Especially if the children are being employed in the service of carbon-offsetting, and thus are
working the land in order to save the planet.

You may be aware, Anon, that there has already been a
child labour/carbon offsetting scandal. It involved David
Cameron. In 2007, newspapers 'exposed' the fact that
Cameron offsets the carbon emitted by his flights around
the world by donating money to a charity that encourages
farmers in India to use treadle pumps instead of diesel-
powered machines. Made from bamboo, plastic and steel,
the treadle pumps work like 'step machines in a gym',
apparently. The farmers pedal for hours in order to draw
up groundwater, which they use to irrigate their farmland.
And because the farming families use 'human energy'
instead of dirty diesel to water their land, each family
saves 0.65 tonnes of carbon a year! Cameron and others
purchase this saved carbon so that they can continue
flying around the world to raise awareness about the

global warming, polar-bear genocide, hurricanes, floods and swarms of locusts that will be unleashed by the unthinking masses of Western societies if they don't stop driving, eating junk food and flying around the world.

Then, some journalist discovered that Indian *children* also use the eco-friendly treadle pumps supported by Cameron. The wide-eyed hack described these kids as 'the carbon-offset child labourers'. Personally, I don't see what all the fuss is about. It's not as if these children are being sent up chimneys to clean away coal stains (yuk!) for tuppence-a-day. No, they are being sent into sunny, green fields to pump Gaia's most beautiful resource – H_2O, which is so much better than CO_2 – on to thirsty crops, *and* they're helping Western eco-activists to continue travelling/living in a super-green fashion.

Anon, everyone I know offsets their carbon by encouraging African and Asian children to carry out some fun and eco-friendly tasks. My friend Zac offsets the carbon costs of all his dinner parties by paying a family of five orphans in Botswana to handpick cotton and make organic-cotton socks which they sell at their local market.

Zac has worked out that each dinner party of his – taking into account the human energy he uses to grow beetroot, turnip, etc, the 'wine miles' used in the transportation of a deliciously sweet and woody red wine from Portugal to Kent, and the amount of tap water it takes to wash his sustainable-wood plates and sustainable-wood cutlery once we're all feeling fat and full – uses 12.2 kg of CO_2. So he spends £4.15 per dinner party on encouraging the Botswana Five (as he calls them!) to pick and stitch organic-cotton products by hand instead of using machinery. The Botswana Five get paid 83p each (which is *a lot* of money in Botswana) and Zac gets to hold a relatively guilt-free dinner do.

Emine and Rafe offset their daughter India's weekly ballet lessons by sponsoring a family of Indian farmers to transport their crops to market ETHICALLY. Eco-aware families have sleepless nights about whether they should allow their daughters to do ballet. There's the *driving* to ballet lessons, which in Emine and Rafe's case uses around 3.2 kg of CO_2 a week, and the fact that ballet shoes are made from *soft leather*, which means ripping the skin from screaming cows just so little girls (and the occasional boy) can swaddle their feet in pink and pirouette and prance around a dance hall.

However, thanks to a wonderfully understanding carbon-offsetting company based here in Kent, Emine and Rafe have found a way to neutralise India's ballet: they sponsor a family in India itself (their daughter's namesake!) to transport their bottles of mango juice to market by donkey rather than by motor-car. So thorough is this Kent-based carbon-offsetting company that it provides LIVE video footage of the family transporting mango juice by donkey, which is beamed directly to India's laptop in her bedroom in Kent. Emine, Rafe and India watch the family walking the seven miles to market every Thursday BEFORE they set out, in peace of mind, on their own journey to Ballet Grade 1.

Easily the most imaginative use of eco-friendly child employment I have heard about was from Sheba's friend,

Abernathy. Abby lives a very ethical life. She's a Stage 10 Vegan (that is, she only eats nuts, seeds or vegetables grown by her own hand and cooked over a very slow heat so they never feel a scalding sensation), and like me she has not been inside a motorised vehicle for more than a decade. However, her one unethical indulgence is using a condom during sexual encounters: well, she doesn't want to contract an STD, or, worse, get pregnant! She offsets her 'sex carbon' – the amount of CO_2 emitted in the production, storage and transportation of the condoms she uses – by sponsoring a group of seven street children in Peru to pick up litter and recycle it as a shantytown dwelling. Through a rather funky carbon-offsetting company called 'Get Your Groove On With A Peruvian!', Abby pays £8.38 every time she has a sexual encounter and the money is given to the seven youthful down-and-outs to construct an abode from discarded cardboard, plastic sheeting, crisp packets and so on. Abby's energetic sex life has paid for an entire shantytown in southern Lima! The locals call it 'Abbytown' – some of the naughtier locals call it 'Shaggytown' . . .

So relax, Anon. And please put the banker's draft for £3.14 that I emailed to you, along with my response to your question, towards your company's Eco-Roundabout Water-Raising Scheme in Sierra Leone. I think it is a superb idea to introduce into the Third World colourful playground roundabouts that double up as pumps for water wells, so that children THINK they're playing and having fun when in fact they are ethically raising drinking water from deep underground for their families! Genius.

☞ **Is it ethical to work in a leisure centre?**

Dear Ethan,
For the past six months I have worked in a lovely
leisure centre in Halifax. I must say it is quite nice to
see people having fun, and working off their angst by
swimming, playing ping pong or exercising in gyms!
But I thought I should check with you that there isn't
something unethical about working in a leisure centre.
I mean, these institutions do not emit anything crazy
like 'sweat carbon', do they?!

Gillian Harper, Halifax

Dear Gillian,

Get out! Get out now! You sound like a nice, possibly even ethical person, so I'm telling you kindly: it is unethical in the extreme to work in, set foot in, or get on a step machine in that Temple to Titillation that is a leisure centre.

What are you thinking, working in a building that is run on a whole town's worth of electricity just so that people can experience *leisure*?! At this moment in time, I can think of no more unethical job than working in a leisure centre. And I'm thinking really, really hard. Pilot? No, not as bad. Pilot on a cheap flight carrying scores of chavs to get wasted in Prague? Maybe. Torturer in a sweaty Egyptian jail cell where kidnapped terror suspects have been rendered and, worse, where energy-guzzling electrical devices will be used to torture them? No – I simply cannot think of anything worse than being a chippy, chirpy, tracksuit-wearing pimp of pleasure in a leisure centre.

From the garishly lit foyer with its refrigerated drinks machines (energy, energy, energy), to the heated swimming pools pumped with chemicals (and children's urine), to the steaming hot showers where buff guys and toned girls stand for MINUTES on end admiring their own freakish and tangoed bodies, a leisure centre is a veritable cathedral of carbon.

Gillian, you must be aware of the research published by the Carbon Trust which revealed that nearly a fifth of the average British citizen's 10.92 tonnes of CO_2 – that is, 1.95 tonnes – is emitted through recreation and leisure? That includes holidaying, going to the gym, and 'enjoying live evening sport under floodlights'. How do you feel now, Gillian, to see your 'lovely' job of working in a leisure centre listed next to WATCHING LIVE SPORT on the unethical Richter scale? I bet you never thought your working day would be spoken about in the same breath as those disgusting gatherings of thousands of grunting men who shout and sweat and drop tonnes of litter as they watch two teams of burly blokes without a GCSE to their names chase a piece of pig's bladder around a muddy field.

Gillian, leisure centres sum up the entire folly of human existence. A leisure centre is an intensive energy-burning institution full of men and women exerting themselves under bright lights and air conditioning outlets, yet it produces nothing! It is a factory-in-reverse, where the masses pile in, work themselves into a sweaty frenzy, and yet have not so much as a box of biscuits or a packet of cigarettes, or whatever else is produced in factories these days, to show for their exertions at the end of it.

However, the fact that leisure centres and gyms are startlingly unethical raises a problem, Gillian – because people DO need to get fitter. There are two very big problems: the first is obviously the expansion of our carbon skidmark across the globe, and the second is the expansion of our waistlines. We face damnation and swarms of locusts courtesy of global warming, and early death by heart attacks courtesy of the obesity epidemic. And these two calamities of gross proportions are directly linked. It's the stuff we do to make ourselves fat – eat junk food, sit around watching *The Jeremy Kyle Show*, drive in jeeps, take flights to France instead of getting there by man-made coracle – that also heats the planet. Fat people cause more discomfort to Gaia than thin people. As a professor at the London School of Hygiene and Tropical Medicine puts it: 'An obese population leaves a significantly heavier footprint than a thin one.'

So how can we get our fat nation fit without allowing them anywhere near an energy-guzzling leisure centre? Well, Gillian, I suggest you give up your eco-irresponsible job quick smart, and set up a Greenhart-style Green Gym.

We Greenharts have devised a circuit-training regime in our back garden. You might call it a Lentil Leisure Centre (zany!) since the circuit training is built around getting fit by planting and harvesting lentils. Step 1: speed-excreting – me, Sheba or one of the kids exert our gluteus maximus, gluteus minimus and gluteus medius (that's the buttocks to the uninitiated) in our outside thermophilic toilet and produce some humanure. Step 2: speed-running – the four of us sprint from the thermophilic toilet carrying the products of step 1 in sustainable-wood egg cups; it's a bit like an egg-and-spoon race but with a whiffy difference! Step 3: speed-spreading – in movements designed to toughen and refine our biceps brachii we hurl the contents of the sustainable-wood egg cups on to the Greenhart allotment where it sinks into the soil and enriches the lentil plants. Step 4: speed-harvesting – in movements aimed at exercising the intertransversarii muscle in our backs, we bend down and pluck the already-grown lentil plants from the soil and sprint back to the house where we make a very well-deserved lentil loaf.

Such circuit-training keeps us AND the planet fit, Gillian, and you should see my gluteus maximus! I am not a vain person, but I do like to show it off in tight-fitting organic-cotton or organic-denim trousers, and if anyone gives me a second glance or wolf-whistle I always make a point of cornering them and explaining in graphic detail that I got this rock-hard butt courtesy of a Green-hart Green Gym where I did my bit for victimised Mother Nature through speed-excreting and speed-plucking. That always wipes the smile off their faces, I find, and also makes them think seriously about the problems facing our planet.

Gillian, you have not a moment to waste! Hand in your notice NOW, disembark from the sinking ship that is human leisure, and construct (from hemp only) a Green Gym where the emphasis should be on people making amends for their sins against the planet through sheer hard graft. I mean, why should we have leisure when Gaia languishes in a steam sauna of our making?

 ## Is it ethical to be an ethical lifestyle columnist?

Dear Ethan,
Like you, we are ethical lifestyle columnists who give advice to the greatly confused people of Great Britain. Unlike you, we write for newspapers rather than the World Wide Web. Does this necessarily make us unethical, though? I mean, you might not use paper and print for your advice columns, but you DO use electricity . . . At the end of the day, is it really ethical for ANYONE to be an ethical lifestyle columnist?
L.S, L.H, A.S, Hampstead, Hampstead, Hampstead

Dear L.S, L.H and A.S,
Ah yes, the million-dollar question: is it ethical to dish out ethical advice?

Now, I am no follower of Jesus Christ. The man was a carpenter for Christ's sake, which means he spent his thirty-three years on what was allegedly 'his Father's planet' chopping down trees and turning them into furniture without, so far as we know, replacing them with *new* trees. But he did have a point when he said: 'Let he who is without sin cast the first stone.' I have always considered ethical column-writing to be the literary equivalent of throwing stones – at the eco-unfriendly, the fat, the feckless, people who deserve it – so it is paramount that those of us who write such columns are without sin. Are we?

L.S, L.H and A.S, cast your minds back to the First National Congress of Ethical Agony Aunts, Agony Uncles and Non-Gender-Specific Advice Dispensers, which was held in London in 2007. What a wonderful day that was! I so enjoyed the ice-breaking activity at the start of the Congress, when we all broke apart some blocks of ice to symbolise the cracking up of Greenland's ice sheets. There were many useful, burning debates, too. I found the discussion on whether it is more ethical for a man to wear Y-fronts or boxer shorts very enlightening, especially the contribution from the ethical adviser from Cardiff, who cut through the tense disagreements in the room over whether organic-cotton underpants are better for Gaia than hemp-based underpants by insisting that Y-fronts are ALWAYS better than boxers because some scientists believe the snug, cloth grip on a man's testicles causes some of his sperm to croak – and thus Y-fronts make men a *little* less fertile, and a *little* less likely to contribute to the overpopulation of the planet. My quite profound column – 'Burn your boxers! Why Mother Earth prefers men in sexy Y-fronts' – sprang from that discussion.

At the end of the Congress, you will recall, we drew up three cardinal rules for our carbon-combating trade, which we decided unanimously to adopt: 1) No carbon shall be emitted in the process of gathering, collating and communicating information aimed at encouraging carbon reduction. 2) All advice shall be communicated in a friendly but stern style, in the manner of a school nurse advising a child with nits how to use a nit comb. 3) Adviser–reader confidentiality is sacrosanct, and under no circumstances should a reader's personal details be publicised (unless you have due cause to believe that he/she is a repeat cheap flyer, in which case you may organise anti-flying protests at their home, place of work and place/s of relaxation).

We all agreed that the most important rule was number one. And I'm afraid, my three (so-called) ethical friends, that if you write for newspapers then you have instantly broken that rule – in fact, you've broken it, ground it down, spat in it and turned it into sludge. Newspapers are to Mother Earth what a lighted match was to Joan of Arc: an inflammatory threat to her continued existence. (That's both literal *and* metaphorical. Newspapers contain *inflammatory* material, such as disgraceful adverts for fast vehicles, fatty foods and other fancy fripperies, and the production of them is likely to *inflame* our planet in a fiery warming the like of which was never envisioned by that eco-unfriendly carpenter from Nazareth.)

Did you know that the *Guardian*, for example, which I know that one of you writes for, purchases 114,000 TONNES of paper a year! Do you know how many trees one must bludgeon, fell, imprison and pulp in order to produce that much paper? No, neither do I. But I know it's a lot. Probably thousands. Maybe tens of thousands. An entire forest, one might say. Then there's the newsprint (chemically produced dyes), the carbon emitted in the production of electricity to power printing presses and the thousands of PCs and laptops used by newspaper journalists, and the petrol guzzled up by the delivery vans that drop piles of these dead trees covered in pointless words at various points around the country.

L.S, L.H and A.S, you accuse me of 'using electricity' in the production of my ethical advice, as if that makes me as bad as you. Well, I can assure you that not so much as a milligram of carbon is emitted during my research and writing. The electricity for my computer is generated entirely by physical labour. We Greenharts have a treadle-pump contraption in the basement, which transforms pedal power into electricity for my laptop. Whenever I need to respond to a query or write my weekly column, my two boys go downstairs and start pedalling – it keeps them in tip-top physical shape and allows me to try (and usually fail) to get the nation into tip-top ethical shape. The boys self-energise themselves, too: if they have to work the treadle pump for long periods of time (they were down there for ten-hour stints while I was compiling this book!), then they urinate into sustainable-wood mugs and Sheba takes their 'output' to our eco-kitchen and mashes it by hand with warm turnip juice to create one of my most muscle-powering drinks, Pee Tea. If my boys are too tired to pedal, or if they go on strike as they once did in 2006 (demanding 'Better Pay, Conditions and Beverages!'), then I simply stop writing. If any of my fans were wondering why I produced not a single word of life-and-death advice between March and May 2006, it's because my boys had smashed the treadle pump in an act of rebellion inspired by the Luddites – which caused me to feel a curious combination of extraordinary pride and extreme anger.

So yes, L.S, L.H and A.S, it *is* ethical to be a lifestyle columnist, if you do it in the eco-proper fashion. I propose that you abandon the newspaper/tree torture world NOW and find carbon-zero ways to tell the nation what kind of underwear to wear, how to grow organic tomatoes, where to buy grape-friendly wine, and other crucially important nuggets of wisdom that might just save Gaia from the coming fiery vortex of doom.

Is it ethical to pray for a recession?

Dear Ethan,
Is there something wrong with me? Every time I read an article or hear a news report about the coming recession, a little part of me jumps for joy. Indeed I find myself thinking, 'Come, recession, come . . .' The rational side of my brain knows it will mean people losing their jobs and possibly their homes . . . but the other side thinks: well, at least it might break our addiction to economic growth! Ethan, is it ethical to pray for a recession?

Maggie Mayfield, Edinburgh, Scotland

Dear Maggie,
If there is something wrong with you, then there's *definitely* something wrong with me. Not only have I prayed

for a recession (to Gaia, of course, not 'God' – yet another arrogant invention of human-unkind who thinks he is so special that a higher being with a beard must have created him!) – I have also *danced* for a recession. Yes, inspired by the beautiful Native American and Maori practice of rain dancing, I have created the 'recession dance'. Where native tribes stamped and grunted to try to coax rain to come and save their crops, I have taken to chanting and humming to try to coax recession to come and save our planet.

Sheba thinks it's mad. But as I said to her, Maggie: 'Is the Dalai Lama mad? Is *Uri Geller* mad? No they aren't, and they know very well the power of thought over real-world events.' I'm very pleased to see that my recession dance is already bearing fruit. I read a report by Reuters recently that says fears of a recession are 'gnawing' at the average American's mindset. Yes!

Maggie, the best thing that could happen to the planet is a recession, a big, beautiful, stock-crashing, Wall Street-burning, consumer-baiting, home-evicting, bank-busting recession. Actually, even better than that would be the emergence of a preferably painless but speedily contagious disease that might finally reduce the human population to sustainable levels – two billion *at the most*, according to my friends in the Optimum Population Trust. But as we wait for a planet-friendly plague that might, in the words of Earth First!, 'bring the human population back to sanity' and 'end industrialism . . . just as the Plague contributed to the demise of feudalism', we will have to make do with economic shocks to our system, with the economic equivalent of the sniffles before the final big disease – the burning of the planet in a fireball created by the greed of the cult of consumers and other lunatics – takes care of 'us' once and for all.

Maggie, the more painful the recession is, the better. Don't worry about people losing their jobs, silly! People who work in banks or shops will be most affected and they deserve everything they get, if you ask me. Banks are parasites on the arse of Gaia, pumping wads of cash into corporations that plunder her resources or build houses (including mock Tudor monstrosities!) on her surface. As for shop assistants or shop managers . . . I'm sorry, but why should we feel sympathy for people who make a living out of sustaining the cancer of consumerism by helping greedy people pick out the latest brand of cookie, car or coat-stand without giving a moment's thought to the billions and billions of trees, plants and natural metals and liquids – Gaia's guts and tears – that will have been sacrificed for their petty pleasures? Worrying about these people losing their jobs is like saying in 1945: 'Oh no, the war's over! What are all those poor little concentration camp guards going to do now?'

The fact is we need *something* to stop us raping the planet, and the recession might just be the chemical castration for the job. We have become so addicted to 'stuff' that anything which reins in consumerism is a good thing. Consider the annual New Year sales, Maggie. All those Burberry-clad product-addicts stamping on each other's heads and stabbing each other with knives – literally sometimes! – as they hunt down the latest kettle or crop top. The consumer society has turned us into savages. Well, not *us* obviously, but certainly *them*: people who think that just because they earn £30,000 a year (they actually think that is a good wage, bless them!), they must spend it all on garish décor and monstrous mod cons for their post-council houses or Barratt eyesores.

On the topic of houses . . . How can you fret that some people might lose their homes?! Have you *seen* these people's homes? Losing them will be the best thing that ever happened to them! With their garish crazy paving and claddagh brick work, their pointless ornaments in the shapes of dogs and penguins (speciesism), their plates and mugs with pictures of Princess Diana or the Queen Mum on them (when we all know that Prince Charles, King of Organic Farming, is the ONLY decent royal), their constantly blaring TVs, radios, computers, DVD players, toasters and tea-makers . . . these houses are more like (very badly decorated) prisons than real homes. If the recession leads to evictions and people have to live more humbly – well, hurrah.

Some psychologists say consumerism and working 24/7 make us mentally ill. Actually, being human is itself a form of mental illness: our brains are programmed to pump various chemicals around our bodies that make us want to fight and destroy and buy, buy, buy. I am confident that evolutionary biologists will shortly discover a gene that triggers the shopping urge. Indeed, a scientist friend of mine (don't worry, he's a *good* scientist – his degree is in Climatalogy, Ecosystems and Industrial Terrorism from the University of South-East Luton) is currently trying to raise funds for his study to discover a

Tesco gene, which he is convinced occurs in malnourished, under-cultured sections of the human race, nurturing in them a pseudo-natural urge to exchange small amounts of money for breadcrumbed chicken legs, strawberry-flavoured milk, copies of *heat* magazine and other bits of Tesco tat. Once we have isolated this gene we can finally use genetic modification for something useful: weeding out brain-dead consumers and workaholic bankers from the human stock.

This is what we're up against, Maggie: beings that are actually *programmed* to destroy, to become poisonous bacteria in Gaia's bloodstream. Let us hope and pray (and dance) that a recession will be the antibody Gaia so desperately needs to deal with her human itch. Maggie, join with me in my recession dance and let us speed in the economic crisis for humankind/happy days for the planet. Contact me for the dancing details.

CARBON ABACUS

If you have ever worked in a supermarket, add 100 beads. If that supermarket was Waitrose take away eighty of those beads; if it was Iceland add a further eighty beads. If a Tesco has been built in your local area and you FAILED to protest against it, add twenty beads.

If you fund eco-friendly child-labour schemes in the developing world, then you may deduct some beads from your final count. If you support the use of primitive and thus ethical farming technology in India, subtract 100 beads. If you support the use of physical labour rather than machinery in cocoa farming in Africa, subtract 100 beads. If you have ever offset a sexual encounter involving the use of eco-unfriendly contraceptives by donating to street children in Latin America, subtract 100 beads.

If you work in a leisure centre, add 100 beads. If you have ever attended a leisure centre for 'leisure', add fifty beads. If you both work in a leisure centre AND make use of its energy-guzzling facilities, add 200 beads. If you have ever swum in a heated pool, add twenty beads. If you urinated in the pool, to teach other regular patrons a lesson about toxins, subtract ten of those beads.

If you are an ethical lifestyle adviser for a newspaper, then stop at once – you really should know better. And add 200 beads.

If you have ever fretted about the coming recession because it will impede your stampede to the shops on a Saturday morning, add fifty beads. If you are a financial analyst who advises people on how to 'survive a recession', shame on you – add sixty beads. If you've never done my Recession Dance, add twenty beads and write to me NOW for the rules of the groove.

Note your bead count here:

. . . .

4

ETHICAL ANIMAL CARE

If you can judge humankind by how we treat our animals, then we're clearly barking mad.

Everywhere I look I see wretched enslaved beasts: dogs on leashes that are only allowed to run free when they're fetching something useless like a stick or a ball for their 'master'; budgerigars in cages driven so demented by imprisonment that they end up squawking phrases from *The Jeremy Kyle Show*; the hides of tortured cows and the severed heads of pigs in shop windows, as if having such gruesome fare on display in the high street is perfectly normal.

And then there are mice. Don't get me started on mice. These poor little bleeders spend every waking hour trying to escape the leather soles of humankind's soulless stamping, or tiptoeing around metal and wooden contraptions designed to snap them in two.

We are suffering from an epidemic of speciesism; indeed, modern society seems to me to be BUILT on the oppression of animals. We wear them on our feet and our backs; tuck into their flesh for breakfast, lunch and dinner; and goad them into performing for us at circuses, greyhound racing tracks, aquariums and various other glorified concentration camps for non-humans.

The ethical life must extend to animals. If you are serious about being seriously ethical, then you must treat animals as equals. That is why our chickens are so free range that they have access to our house as well as our garden. When Sheba complains about chicken poop on her pillow, I tell her it is a small price to pay for treating animals with respect.

I have also instilled these values into my children. They have brought home stray dogs, stray cats, ferrets, rats, injured crows, toads, mink and even a tarantula! And every one of these creatures becomes an equal member of the Greenhart family, instantly awarded dinner-table rights, bedroom rights and family-meeting voting rights.

If you do not treat animals ethically, you are an unethical animal – plain and simple. Digest this chapter immediately.

 ## Is it ethical to trap mice?

Dear Ethan,
We have mice in our house! I need to get rid of them.
They keep leaving droppings everywhere, and because I
am an eco-sensitive kind of guy I just know I will flip
out and SCREAM if I see one of the creatures
scurrying about! But I don't want to hurt them. Is
there an ethical way to get rid of mice?
*   Jimmy Westerley, Glasgow*

Dear Jimmy,
'Get rid' of the mice?! And you call yourself an 'eco-sensitive kind of guy'!? There is no ethical way to 'get rid' of mice because it is a completely unethical thing to do.

Jimmy, if you can de-clutter your brain of its culturally programmed notions of human superiority for just five minutes, then you might like to put yourself in the mouse's position. (There is a brilliant workshop in a community centre in Finchley, north London, called 'Be The Mouse' which encourages humans to 'regress' – I prefer to call it '*progress*' – to the mental and physical state of a mouse, by squeaking instead of speaking and getting down on all fours and pooing in the corner of the room.) Imagine how horrendous and hard life is for mice who set up a lovely little nest in 'your' home – because we humans have poisoned *their* home, the countryside – only to be deafened by the sounds of your hoover and TV, overheated by the boiling water that streams through your central heating pipes, and threatened by the constant stamping of your clumpy boots and shoes made from the stolen hides of murdered cows. People claim to be scared of mice, but it's the mice who exist in a permanent state of staring, wide-eyed terror.

You know what really gets my goat? (Arrgh, I hate that speciesist phrase! What do we mean *my* goat? Goats are not ours to own.) It is when people complain about mouse droppings. So a mouse leaves a few odourless, cylindrical droppings here and there – big deal. That is nothing compared with the tonnes of shit that sixty-five million Brits pass every day, which flows from our toilets into massive stinking sewers that are a terrible testament to the wastefulness of human life.

Many a dinner party *chez* Greenhart has been ruined by mice. No, not by the creatures themselves – they would be more than welcome to join us, only we usually don't eat cheese because it's a dairy product; sorry, mice. Rather, the *soirée* is spoilt by heated debates about how to deal with mice. We all know that the old-fashioned mousetrap, one of the most foul inventions of the modern era, is an affront to animalkind: an agonising, back-snapping, body-spiking weapon that makes Mme Guillotine seem positively humane. But, Jimmy, the various 'ethical' ways to trap mice are a big no-no, too.

Some green-minded souls go for the RADAR – the Rodent Activated Detection and Riddance device. Apparently this is the world's 'smartest mousetrap', but like everything that 'smart' humans do – industrialisation, anyone? – it is actually pretty horrific. A mouse enters a specially made box, duped inside by the promise of food, and then the door shuts behind him. A tiny canister releases carbon dioxide; in ten seconds the mouse is out cold, and in sixty seconds it is dead. This 'clever' device then automatically sends an email to a pest controller to let him know that a mouse has been trapped and 'painlessly' killed. Hmmm, a living creature shoved into a chamber and gassed to death . . . sound familiar?

One friend of mine boasted at a recent BYOB (Bring Your Own Beetroot) party that he uses the most humane method of all to 'get rid' of mice. He lays down the Trap Man Humane Mousetrap, which traps the mouse and even feeds and waters it until the home 'owner' comes home and finds it. Then you take the trapped mouse to a field and set it free. Hurrah? Not quite. First of all, what gives humans the right to falsely imprison mice? Second of all, do you know what happens to mice when they are rumbled away from their rightful homes and ditched in a distant field? Yep, they die – and so do the families they leave behind in 'your' home.

Jimmy, you have only two options. First, you may try the Pied Piper Method. This involves using a recorder (made from renewable wood, otherwise the whole exercise is null and void) to entice the mice to follow you to a *safe* environment. I and the kids tried this once: we faced down Sheba's warnings that the neighbours would think we're stone mad and piped and jigged our way from the front door to a nearby field. Unfortunately, the mice did not follow. Clearly, even a soothing melody cannot make them overcome their fear and loathing for humankind.

Your second option – and the one I most strongly recommend – is to get rid of *yourself*. Remove yourself and your family from the house, and let the mice live in peace. This, however, might put a strain on your marriage. When I set up a Mouse Liberation Caravan in our backyard a couple of years ago, and moved the family into it so that the family of mice in our cottage could enjoy their short time on this poisoned planet, Sheba packed her bags and stayed at her mother's. I can only hope that the comment she made as she left – 'I'm not coming back till you kill every single one of the bastards with a steel trap or let me skewer them with the heel of my Jimmy Choos!' – popped out in the heat of the moment and was later regretted. No matter – temporary separation of man and wife is a small price to pay for the tear-inducing symbolism of handing one's home over to some of Gaia's weakest and most defenceless creatures.

In the end, Sheba and I compromised: we moved back to the cottage and the mice moved into the caravan along with their ratty friends, until someone from the totally misnamed 'environmental' health department forced us to get rid of our sanctuary-on-two-wheels on the basis that it was 'shockingly unsanitary'. Trust government officials to see a halfway home for between 200 and 250 mice, rats and ferrets, which is what our Mouse Liberation Caravan eventually became, as 'unsanitary'.

Never forget, Jimmy, that the 'pests' who really need to be controlled are we humans, and the 'vermin' who ought to be exterminated are you, me and the other six billion full-time excretors on the planet. Forget mousetraps – we need some man traps. Or, actually, maybe we just need *more* mice. Wasn't it our dear little friends who helped to spread plagues in centuries gone by? Such mouse ingenuity and solidarity with nature, which helped to wipe out a third of Europe's destructive human population during the Black Death, are sorely needed again today.

Is it ethical to take my children to the zoo?

Dear Ethan,
Like you, I have two children – and like you I plant thirty-two trees per child per year in order to offset their existences. So please be aware, before you read my question, that I AM an ethical person! What I want

to know is this: is it ethical to take my children to a zoo? They have been begging me for years, and I have always said 'No' on the basis that zoos are rotten human inventions. Am I right? Or should I give in to the kids?

Surinder Khan-Wheatley, Cardiff

Dear Surinder,

I know what you think I'm going to say – that nobody should ever set foot inside a zoo, and in an ideal world zoos would be nuked (if only nukes themselves weren't so darn eco-unfriendly). In fact, I think taking littl'uns to the zoo is an EXCELLENT idea. After all, what better way could there be to educate one's offspring about how sinister and foul humanity is than by taking them to an animal concentration camp, to a place where we incarcerate elephants, make a mockery of monkeys, and charge people a couple of quid to sit between the humps of a depressed camel? A trip to the zoo is a marvellous educational experience for a growing ethically-aware child.

Sheba and I take our two kids to London Zoo once a month. We call it Animal Suffering Awareness Day. The first thing we do once inside the prison gates is try to raise the awareness of families less ethical than the Greenharts. We start by setting up a 'human enclosure'. Sheba and I rapidly construct a cage from bamboo shoots, which I sneak into the zoo in my organic-sackcloth backpack. Our kids get inside the cage and we post an information sign next to them:

Modern human: a bipedal primate that belongs to the mammalian species Homo sapiens (Latin for 'wise man' or 'knowing man'; ironic). Possesses highly developed brain capable of abstract reasoning, introspection and language (usually foul). Brain mainly used for thinking up new ways to destroy own natural environment. Mostly found across Europe, the Americas, Asia, Africa, Australasia, but thankfully not so much in Antarctica. Do not feed. They're quite obese enough already.

We leave this enclosure up for one hour, to give the families streaming into the zoo some serious food for thought. The kids nearly died of embarrassment when a group of their friends from Kent turned up at the zoo and saw them in the enclosure. 'Why do you make us *do* these things?' asked my red-faced eldest boy. I told him he was doing it for Gaia, not for me, and if his so-called 'friends' did not understand then maybe it was time for him to get some new friends – or forswear human friends altogether in favour of animal companionship, which is what I did when I was his age, and I turned out just fine.

After dismantling our human enclosure, we try to drum up support for our ethical tour of the zoo, what we call the Alternative Route through Zoo Enclosures (ARZE). Sheba and I lead it, with our kids in tow, and the families who follow our ARZE get a wonderful treat: a glimpse at the dark underbelly of zoo life. Cleverly, during the tour I never refer to *enclosures* but rather to *cells*! And instead of saying *zoo* I say *prison camp*! Such a subtle change in lingo really pricks people's consciences – I actually hear a lot of mums and dads using the word 'prick' as I guide them through the hellish existences of dejected giraffes, lonely hippopotamuses, and bats driven even battier than usual by having to flap around in a tiny, enclosed space instead of being allowed to fly freely above our heads and, yes, to get tangled in our hair or suck on our blood if they really want to. One sad bat looked longingly at my neck through the thick pane of glass, through the disgraceful barrier erected by the zoo authorities between a beast and its prey, between the bat and my bloodstream. Surinder, I was so sorely tempted to smash the glass and to offer my neck – nay, my entire body! – to the colony of bats, thus sacrificing myself in a flapping orgy of blood-and-flesh recycling where my very personhood would become bat urine and poo and seep into and enrich the soil that is Gaia's coating! But I resisted. Sheba could tell what I was thinking and gave me the evil eye. And I did promise her after the Lizard Liberation incident during our last ARZE at London Zoo that I would NOT break the law in a zoo setting ever again. Sorry, bats.

When our ARZE comes to a close, we carry out the most important educational protest of Animal Suffering Awareness Day: we head towards the face-painting stall. How that institution fills me with horror, Surinder! The sight of parents lining their children up so that they can be painted in garish colours as a tiger or flamingo or giraffe makes the lentil loaf leap in my stomach! We all frown upon 'blacking up' these days, yet we seem to think it's OK to 'animal up'; we rightly reel back in disgust if anyone dresses up as a black-and-white minstrel or a ginger-haired leprechaun, yet we think it's OK to prance around like a second-rate anteater. The face-painting stall at the zoo tells you everything you need to know about human hubris: our 'me, me, me' culture is captured in the queue of selfish toddlers waiting to be dolled up, and our unashamed speciesism comes through in the arrogant notion that we have the right to impersonate – or perhaps im*animal*ate – our fellow mammals, birds and fish.

In protest, we Greenharts first wave placards saying, 'FACE IT – FACE-PAINTING IS FOUL'; judging by the number of kids who cry when they see us, this is a very effective and emotional slogan. Then we set up an Alternative Face-Painting stall to represent those poor beasts who are not an option at the zoo's official face-painting stall. At our stall you can become a tarantula, a great white shark or a lemming – three beautiful animals that have been libelled by humankind as psychotic killers and suicide cases. Do any of the kids come to our stall? Do they hell-on-earth!

See, Surinder, there are plenty of ethical and educational larks to be had at a zoo. So take your children there NOW – and, using humour and funny colourful props, open their eyes to the unbelievable horror that is a sprawling Auschwitz for animals.

☛ Is it ethical to muzzle dangerous dogs?

Dear Ethan,
As a social worker, I occasionally have to venture on to council estates and into inner-city urban enclaves.

While there, I always see lots of muzzled 'dangerous dogs'. The owners of these dogs are required by the authorities to keep a leather muzzle over the poor beasts' mouths. Surely this is unethical? Would I be justified in giving in to my temptations and ripping the muzzles off these dogs, thus allowing them to bark and bite freely?

Abel Hartley, Hyde Park

Dear Abel,

You're right: such muzzling is a crime against canine-kind. I know many human beings who spend their every waking hour talking complete and utter tosh – should we muzzle them, too? Indeed, on some of the council estates you describe, there usually lives a class of human being known as the Football Hooligan. These large men have shaven heads and sport crude tattoos – not ethically interesting tattoos of willow trees and whistling birds, like the one sported by Sheba on her left shoulder, but tattoos of grinning bulldogs and faded Union Jacks. They are renowned for their irrational violent outbursts, which can even include biting people! So why don't we muzzle them, and tie their legs together to stop them kicking others with their Doc Martens, and surgically remove their tongues while we're at it so that their foul and nationalistic language can no longer pollute the cultural environment in the same way that their beer-heavy urine and discarded kebabs pollute the urban environment?

If we were to muzzle humans there would be an outcry from civil libertarians. Well, I am declaring myself a 'canine libertarian', who will cry out on behalf of down-trodden dogs.

Of course, it's always tragic when a dog lashes out and bites its owner or an unsuspecting child. But let's get one thing straight: these 'dangerous dogs' are not expressing any warped 'animal instinct': they're merely an extension of their owners' disgusting human instincts. As Sue Carroll, a columnist for the *Daily Mirror*, so aptly put it, if we are going to muzzle 'dangerous dogs' then we should muzzle their 'vile owners', too. Carroll described the average pit bull owner as a 'feckless Neanderthal' on an 'inner-city estate' with 'no concept of restraint or judgement'. She's so right.

Jon Snow, the green-leaning, bike-riding, *Guardian*-reading presenter of Channel 4 News, who I'm sure would be my favourite newsreader if I actually owned a TV and believed it was legitimate for humankind to organise 'world events' in a hierarchical order and label them 'newsworthy' (which I most certainly do not), once said: 'It is one of life's great unexplained peculiarities that people like to provide a home for violent uncontrollable animals as if in some way these beasts fulfil some animal instinct of their own.' He's on the money there: the real animals are the owners of 'dangerous dogs', who use and abuse these poor beasts to satisfy their own diabolical urges.

But we must stop speaking in code. When people talk about 'Neanderthals' with 'animal instincts', we know what they are really referring to: whisper it . . . the U-word. Well, Abel, I am going to break the last taboo in the politics of ethical living and say it out loud: it's the underclass, stupid!

Too many environmentalists use guarded language these days. Let's say what we really mean! When we write about those awful 'zombies' who unthinkingly shop at T****, we mean working-class and underclass families who cannot be bothered to grow their own fruit and veg. When we write about people who take cheap flights, we mean clinically obese individuals from social classes D, E and F who holiday in Prague or Riga where they consume and then vomit up vast quantities of warm lager and alcopops. And when we talk about Neanderthals, we mean the inhabitants of inner-city estates who wear falling-down jeans and baseball caps and who wouldn't know what a recycling bin was if one landed on their heads.

The underclasses are more polluting than we better-educated middle classes, Abel. I know this to be a fact because when I was studying for my degree in Environmental Theory I carried out an on-the-ground study of a council estate on the outskirts of Kent. This is actually when I first met Sheba: she was taking the same course as me, and we joined forces for an end-of-term study on 'The Impact of Impoverished Living and Impoverished Morality on the Quality of Air and Integrity of Ecosystems'. We went undercover to see how underclass communities impact on the natural environment. I adopted the name Dave, pronounced 'Daaayve', and wore the fashionable underclass uniform of the day: shell suit and sneakers. Sheba adopted the name Chelsea, pronounced 'Chel-seee', and wore a pink tracksuit top, revealing mini-skirt, and staggeringly high high-heels. We spent three days on the estate, and what we saw was extraordinary.

There were people SMOKING and, worse, littering the streets with their fag butts. There were people using toxin-based spray-paint to write obscene messages on brick walls such as 'Paul is a grass', 'Fuck tha police', and 'Dave and Chelsea are twats'. There were people eating chips from newspapers, and then THROWING THE NEWSPAPERS ON THE GROUND! And yes, they treated their dogs – invariably named Tyson or Leatherface – awfully.

Using carbon abacuses, we discovered that an average member of the underclass emits 7.2 tonnes of carbon a year compared with the 4.8 tonnes emitted by an average member of the middle classes. We concluded our study by arguing: 'There must be a concerted effort to change the behaviour and lifestyle of poorer members of British society, in order to wean them away from eco-terroristic habits and to transform them into responsible guardians of urban ecosystems.' We wrote those words in 1991! I'm so pleased to see that, since then, green campaigners have indeed focused most of their efforts on tackling the pollution caused by 'Tesco shoppers', 'cheap flyers' and 'dangerous dog owners' – or what I still insist on calling, rather bravely in my view, the unfortunate underclass.

Abel, I must advise you AGAINST taking it upon yourself to remove the muzzles from 'dangerous dogs' – not because the dogs might bite you, but because their owners might. Instead, why not join my canine libertarian campaign to have the violent *human* thugs in inner-city

Britain muzzled, so that more people like you and me might feel less scared to venture into these urban moral vacuums and begin the mammoth task (with apologies to mammoths) of re-educating the reprobates in the ways of ethical living?

☞ **Is it ethical to keep a cow as a pet?**

Dear Ethan,
Help! I have two cows – Al and Gore – in my back garden. I love them dearly. But now we're told that cows, with their methane-based farting and belching, contribute more carbon to the environment than CARS! What should I do? Kill my cows and eat them, which would at least mean bringing to an end their methane terror and also recycling their bodily matter as excrement and compost? Please advise!
Shelly Montgomery, Watford

Dear Shelly,
Ah yes, cows and their nasty methane. I've seen all those smug reports which claim that 'Cows Not Cars are to Blame for Global Warming'. It's true that cows, like all living creatures, produce methane, a by-product of the action of bacteria breaking down ingested food matter. And it's true that because cows have four stomachs (see how much more evolved they are than we one-stom-ached humans?), they create considerably more of the gas than any other earthly beast. As a consequence of their grassy farting, cows contribute 18 per cent of all

greenhouse gas emissions, which is significantly more than cars.

But don't fall for the simplistic 'cows are polluters' line, Shelly, and don't kill off Al and Gore just yet.

The focus on polluting cows is part of what I like to call the 'Cows Cause Climate Change Con', or the 'Great Cattle-Blaming Swindle'. The 'cows are worse than cars' argument has allowed every carbon fascist and climate change denier – you know who you are – to say: 'Ha, those tree-hugging pansies have got it all wrong! Animals are the problem, not humans!' Well, this tree-hugging pansy has got news for the carbon mafia: the cows' contribution to climate change is ALSO OUR FAULT. It is our meaty greed, our bloodlust for flesh, that has led to the enslavement of millions of cows who have no choice but to graze on cheap grass or man-made chemicalised feed so that they can get fat for the culinary pleasure of a family of fat humans. We have turned cows into machines – I'm almost weeping as I write this! – and like all machines they emit noxious gases that damage the environment.

As the owner of two cows, you will know how special they are, Shelly, despite what people who suffer from cattlephobia might claim. The second most shocking thing that ever appeared on TV (after Martin Durkin's Channel 4 film, *The Great Global Warming Swindle*, obviously) was a stand-up gig by the comedian Lee Evans. I didn't actually see it, of course, since I haven't caught a glimpse of a TV image since I accidentally spied something called *EastEnders* while walking past a Dixon's in 1998. But I heard about it. Apparently Evans said: 'People say, why do we kill so many cows? Because they're *crap*! They have no survival instincts whatsoever. They're dumb animals, otherwise they would learn to shit without it hitting the back of their legs.'

I wrote to Ofcom. I demanded to know why it is forbidden to insult ethnic minorities on TV but it's OK to call a cow a dumb animal. I got no reply – yet further evidence that Britain is riddled with Institutionalised Speciesism.

Of course, all forms of farming are vile and corrupt. The cultivation of land and beast for the benefit of human stomachs is built on the idea that man has a RIGHT to use and abuse the planet! But cattle farming is the worst: the evidence shows that breeding cows and keeping them prisoner damages the environment with methane as well as being barbaric, so it's time we took two urgent steps. First, we must outlaw mass meat farming. For too long, farmers have pumped animals with chemicals and genes and sprinkled the Devil's dust (pesticides) on to their crops. Industrial farming, like foxhunting, smoking in public places and making fun of religion, should be outlawed NOW! Where is New Labour's zeal for banning things when we need it most?

Second, we must put pressure on the government to extol the benefits of vegetarianism. We must wean the masses off their addiction to junk meat – those jumbo burgers that are a jumbled mix of flesh and bone and beak and claw. Many incentives can be used to 'force' (I know, I don't like that word either, but what can you do?) people to go vegetarian. For example, it's been mooted that doctors should not treat smokers because they bring on their own ill-health. Well, how about withholding healthcare from carnivores who clog up their own arteries and veins because they cannot resist wolfing down a leg that has been ripped from a chicken and dipped in acidy fat?

There is an irony in my demand for state-sanctioned vegetarianism: we veggies are known to fart quite a lot, too! Just ask Sheba. So, isn't it time we developed innovative ways to harness OUR wind and turn it into energy? I propose putting a fart box in every home, a contraption that would capture our leaking methane and turn it into gases with which we can warm our homes, work our ovens and energise our gadgets.

I have already experimented in this area, Shelly. I have installed a Methane Recycling Unit built by a friend of mine who works in eco-engineering. When my two kids need to fart, they do it into a long plastic tube that leads to an air-tight canister. Here, their methane is separated from the less useful content of human wind and is transformed into energy. This energy is used specifically for the children's electrical devices – in particular their PlayStation. We have discovered that a week's worth of farting creates one minute's worth of electrical power. And because the children are ONLY allowed to use methane to power their PlayStation, they have found all sorts of ways to make themselves fart more often! They have stashes of baked beans in their rooms, and where once they dry-heaved at the sight of my wind-inducing lentil loaves, now they tuck into them with demented abandon. Some know-it-all at Social Services might call this 'child neglect', after my youngest boy collapsed in school and then spent fifteen-and-a-half minutes farting in the nurse's office. I prefer to call it 'children taking some responsibility for eco-friendly energy creation', thank you very much.

Shelly, leave Al and Gore to their joyous life in your back garden, forget about their farting, and ask yourself this: what are YOU doing to transform your own windy-pops into something useful?

👉 Is it ethical to eat a chicken, ever?

Dear Ethan,
I don't mind telling you that I'm confused! Lots of celebrity chefs are talking about the horror of cheap, battery-farmed chickens and calling on the British public to eat organic, free-range chickens instead. But surely it is unethical to eat any kind of chicken? Or am I out of step? Is it OK to eat a properly reared chicken from Waitrose? If so, please let me know – I haven't had chicken in 17 years, and I'm rather peckish for one!

June Shay, Oxford

Dear June,
Oh yes, that's fine. Feel free to walk into your local Waitrose and pick up a beautifully basted chicken for your dinner tonight. While you're out and about you

might also like to buy a canister of oil from your local petrol station and douse its contents over a family of unsuspecting ancient oaks, kick a few dogs into the middle of the road so that they can get squished by a blinged-up, big-haired Chelsea mum motoring along in her 4x4 killing-machine, and book some cheap flights to Riga so that you and your family can leave a carbon skidmark in the sky (and a literal skidmark on that misfortunate city's streets) as you enjoy a drink-fuelled, carbon-filled, vomit-stained lads' and ladettes' holiday from hell.

June, WHAT ARE YOU THINKING?! Eat a chicken?!! What if I wrote you a letter saying: 'Dear June. I don't mind telling you that I'm confused! Everyone talks about how cute and wonderful children are, yet I have an insatiable, burning, stomach-rumbling desire to EAT one of yours. Any recipe recommendations? Toddler a l'Orange? Breadcrumbed baby legs with a side of potato salad and rocket leaves?'

Shocking, right? Well, I have news for you, June: chickens are people too. They have feelings and emotions and aspirations for their offspring that are somewhat higher than ending up on a drooling carnivore's dinner plate, and later inside his guts, and even later inside the sewer system alongside the rest of the dung, discarded condoms and murdered funfair goldfish that humanity flushes away every day.

Now, don't get me wrong. I think that in raising awareness about battery farming, celeb chef Hugh Fearnley-Whittingstall has done the nation a favour. I know, I know, he is a fully paid up meat-eater, who has even shockingly suggested that people should scoop up 'roadkill' (dead squirrels, badgers, birds and the like) and take it home to cook, as if those poor buggers hadn't suffered enough at the hands of human-unkind. (I prefer to call the bulging-eyed beasts that blood-stain our highways 'roadmurder', and to bury them in extravagant ceremonies that praise Gaia and curse car-kind. Sheba thinks it's bad for the kids to make them wear black and chant in the middle of a forest while surrounded by dead animals, especially since some silly social worker in Kent has got it into her head that the kids and I are involved in a wacky Satanist cult.)

Anyway, a roadkill-scraper he may be, but Fearnley-Whittingstall has at least educated us about one important thing: anyone who buys cheap meat from big, evil super-markets (no, not Waitrose or Sainsbury's – the OTHER one) is a disgusting specimen of a human being who clearly thinks nothing of inflicting pain on animals to satisfy his lust for meat and probably cannot even spell the word 'ethical'.

Fearnley-Whittingstall's work follows on neatly from the efforts of a close friend of mine, Rocco Montague-De Bounevialle-Wagner, who is also an organic farmer (a VEGETARIAN one). As Montague-De Bounevialle-Wagner points out in his forthcoming book *Chicken Holocaust: Why Cheap Meat is the Crime of the Century*, ALL meat-eaters are bad, but cheap meat-eaters – those who buy two dead chickens for a fiver! – are the lowest of the low, beyond redemption and probably even beyond re-education, the modern-day equivalent of cannibalistic savages (well, their intellect is likely to be on a par with a chicken's, if not lower, so why shouldn't we call their chicken-gobbling 'cannibalism'?). Montague-De Bounevialle-Wagner's solution, to tackle the epidemic of cheap meat-eating, is as clear as it is principled and gallant: the government must increase its subsidies to small organic farmers like Montague-De Bounevialle-Wagner and Fearnley-Whittingstall by 5,000 per cent and introduce strict trade laws that forbid supermarkets from selling broiler chickens, battery-produced eggs or factory-farmed milk in order to put Big Farmers out of business.

Rocco's right. Even I, a black belt vegan, who doesn't eat anything that ever had a face, a pulse, a relationship to the sun that involved physical bending (a sure sign of sentience), or the ability to flower, can concede that there is 'good meat' and 'bad meat'. We can leave the war on 'good meat' to one side for the time being. It is those who eat 'bad meat' – cheap chickens, turkey twizzlers, chipolatas submerged in a tin of barbecue-flavoured baked beans (!!) – who must be challenged/sectioned. If it isn't bad enough that they tend to be under-educated in the first place, and then to have whatever education they did receive hounded out of them by the brain-frying monotony of a zombie job in a supermarket or on a car assembly line, on top of that their brain cells and cerebral nerve-ends are frazzled even further by the stodgy and poisonous grub they consume! They live in a vicious cycle: they eat cheap chicken because they're a bit thick – and then the cheap chicken makes them a bit more thick.

We need to take action now. The government must set up Food Monitoring Committees to assess what people store in their fridges and feed to their children. It is not enough to have Hugh Fearnley-Whittingstall – or even Rocco Montague-De Bounevialle-Wagner (good luck with your Channel 4 proposal *What Your Poo Says About You*, Rocco!) – on TV telling everyone to get a grip. That still leaves room for people to make choices, and they always, without fail, as predictably as lemmings on a cliff edge, make the wrong choices. No, we need to police what supermarkets sell, police what people buy, police what they eat, and if necessary police their poo – Gillian McKeith-style – to ensure that they aren't LYING about their weekly eating habits.

I, for one, will volunteer for the front line of the sewer system, magnifying glass in hand, if it means catching those meat-eaters red-handed, or perhaps red-bottomed, who have told the food-policing authorities a few pork pies (pun intended). Only then, June, might we wipe meat out of the human system and return some of humanity, at least, to its senses.

CARBON ABACUS

If you have ever used a mousetrap, add 300 beads. Please also stop reading my book. I am not at all comfortable with the thought of a mouse-killer engaging with my ideas. If you have used any other method to kill/trap/dispense with a mouse, add twenty beads.

If you have ever visited a zoo for fun, add 100 beads. If you have ever visited a zoo to educate your children about the innate wickedness of humankind, pat yourself on the back.

If you own a dangerous dog, how are you managing to read these words? Is someone reading them to you? If so, please tell that person to add 100 beads for owning a dangerous dog and a further 200 beads if you have ever muzzled it.

If you keep a cow in your garden and allow it to run free, well done. If you keep a cow on a farm and allow it to run free but will one day kill it and eat it, add 100 beads. If you keep a cow in a cage with a milking machine attached to its udders, and plan shortly to stun it, shoot it and carve it up, add 1,000,000 beads. If you have ever made a joke about a cow, or pushed one over in a field to see it fall down, add 200 beads.

If you have ever eaten a chicken burger, beefburger, cheeseburger, ostrich burger, crocodile burger or any other class of burger, add fifty beads.

Note your bead count here:

. . . .

5

ETHICAL TRANSPORT

Once upon a time, humankind had no choice but to stay put. We rarely went beyond our garden gate and never travelled from one country to another. Journeys were tiresome, exhausting and demeaning: they usually involved sitting in the back of a carriage while a horse or donkey dragged you over bumpy unpaved roads, and having to cover your snout with a hankie to keep at bay the whiff of manure and the stench of olden-day life in general.

Those were the days! People knew their place, and they stayed there. Now we all want to 'broaden our horizons'. Which sounds quite fancy and promising, until you realise that it means broadening one's carbon skidmark, too.

Most of YOUR carbon emissions probably come out of an exhaust pipe. We happily cough and choke black smog into Mother Earth's pristine face just so long as it gets us from A to B – and then on to C, D and E, too. And if driving cars and motorbikes and hopping on buses with abandon were not bad enough, there is also the dreaded aeroplane . . . probably the worst invention of all time ever. After the wheel, of course, which facilitated all this travelling around in the first place. Could ancient man ever have known that his simple round device designed to move heavy loads from one cave to another would later be used to move cars and trucks along roadways and planes screeching across runways? If only some ancient brainbox had never had that bloody idea.

There are, as always, bad forms of modern transport and even worse forms of modern transport. Driving, getting a train, getting on and off buses, flying to Mongolia – that's all pretty bad. But then there are CHEAP FLIGHTS, which are without question the bane (and the pain) of Mother Earth's half-life.

These monstrous inventions allow EVERYONE to fly overseas! That means Gaia is being polluted not only so that a clever professor and his smartly dressed wife can visit catacombs in Rome, but also so that a road-digger and his 'bird' can go salsa dancing in Barcelona. People whose forefathers never ventured farther than the edge of the town (because they could not afford the very sensible road toll enforced by local sheriffs, and besides, had nowhere to go) are now jetting around the world as if they owned it.

In this chapter, read about the mucky horrors of modern transport, and the virtues of remaining perfectly still forever.

Is it ethical to use force to stop people flying?

Dear Ethan,
I'm a young eco-campaigner truly DISGUSTED by
flying. People just don't understand how harmful their

*holidaymaking is for the rest of the planet. I spent a
week at the Climate Action Camp in Heathrow in
August 2007. I dressed up as Death – with long black
cloak and scythe! – and shouted at families of
holidaymakers in the duty free shops: 'Thank you for
flying abroad and as a consequence killing the planet.
It keeps me (that is, Death) very busy!' Amazingly,
even this creative form of protest did not make them
change their minds about flying abroad. Ethan, what
can we do to ground all flights once and for all? Is it
ethical to use force to stop people from flying?*

Jonty DeMontfort, Harrow, Middlesex

Dear Jonty,
I'm so pleased that young people like you are taking a
stand against the evil aviation industry and the unthinking
holidaymakers who patronise it. I have sleepless nights
thinking about the carbon footprint – nay, the carbon
bootprint; nay, the carbon nuclear-style mushroom – that
is left on our vulnerable planet by the herds of horrible
holidaymakers who think that floods, hurricanes, pestilence and poverty are a price worth paying so they can top
up their tans and win the 'I'm the brownest!' competition
among a gaggle of Vicky Pollards at their local beercan-
littered bus-stops. We MUST do something about the
stag-night drunks who stain Prague with their puke, the
fat families who waddle around the beaches of southern
Spain in ill-fitting flip-flops, and the slags (I'm sorry but
there is no other word for them) who teeter on white high-
heels through the streets of Faliraki on the lookout for

cheap booze and even cheaper sex. Their ceaseless flying farts out so many toxins that they are as guilty of MURDER as surely as if they had suffocated that poor African family at risk from floods/drought with their own coarse, manual labour hands.

Flying is without a shadow of a doubt the worst thing that any human being could ever do, EVER. Sheba said to me recently: 'Ethe, I've just been reading the *Economist* and it says the aviation industry contributes only 3 per cent of the world's total carbon emissions, way behind factories.' I barked back at her: 'So? What's your point?' She replied: 'My point is: don't these figures rather undercut your irrational fury about flying, and more importantly might we now take that trip to Tuscany I've been begging you for?' I saw red, Jonty! What Sheba doesn't understand is that, yes, flying might be a relatively minor emitter of carbon . . . but it emits carbon in the name of people having FUN!

Holidays, especially cheap holidays facilitated by cheap flights and enjoyed by cheap people (social classes D, E and F), are fundamentally unnecessary. My carbon abacus tells me that every stag night in Prague – taking into account return flights for eight people, the cleaning products required to remove their vomit from the streets, and the impact of their discarded non-biodegradable condoms on the local water supply – causes 1.4 per cent of a hurricane in Bangladesh. So it takes only 71.4 stag nights to cause a full hurricane in Bangladesh! Is that a price worth paying just so you can get off your trolley and drop your trousers in Wenceslas Square?

Anyone who flies is complicit in crimes against the planet – or what I call *Grimes* Against Humanity. One ethical newspaper columnist argues that man-made flight is causing death and destruction on a scale that will make 'genocide and ethnic cleansing look like side-shows at the circus of human suffering'. It's so true! Well, not literally true, of urse, but metaphorically true. And if flying is metaphorically worse than genocide, then holidaymakers are metaphorically worse than Hitler: these genocidAIRes must be prevented from taking Aryan-air or eaSSyjet flights overseas.

Jonty, it seems obvious to me that the first concrete step (yuk, I hate that phrase! Why should a positive step forward be described as 'concrete'?) towards stopping flying is to bring in a Flight Offenders Register. Modelled on the Sex Offenders Register, this central-government file will record the details of every person who flies anywhere for any reason. It is impossible to re-educate the sun monsters and booze-hounds who jet abroad without a moment's consideration for Gaia – because they are a) usually drunk and b) brainwashed by garish 'Come to Turkey' adverts – but we can NAME AND SHAME THEM. The Flight Offenders Register should be available for viewing to everyone, so that you find out if a repeat flier is living near you.

The second 'concrete step' we can take is to *raise taxes* on all flights of distances more than ten miles (thus not unnecessarily punishing eco-friendly hang-gliders). I have learned that the average family in social classes D, E and F sets aside £600 for their annual holidays. We must therefore tax flights to the tune of £650 and finally price out the most destructive flyers, saving the skies from their carbon and blocks of frozen pee and the streets of once-beautiful towns in Greece and Spain from their foul language and warm fresh pee.

Once these hucksters have been expelled from the skies, we can turn our attention to winding down holidays taken by eco-tourists – yes, Margo and Zac, I am thinking of you! I KNOW your annual educational igloo-building trips to Alaska are well-intentioned; I KNOW that you offset the carbon cost of your flights by donating to a charity that encourages farmers in Bangladesh to use treadle pumps instead of diesel pumps to irrigate their land with water; and I KNOW that this gives rise to a beautiful symmetry of interests between the developing world and the developed world, where African farmers work by hand and you use the 2.7 tonnes of carbon saved as a result to facilitate a trip to rub noses with Inuits and immerse yourselves and your beautiful adopted Chinese children in the Inuit culture of ice-utilisation, sustainable fishing and ethical fire-starting. BUT . . . you are setting a bad example to less well-informed people in social classes D, E and F!

The third 'concrete step' we can take, Jonty, is to carry out more *creative protests*. Dressing up as Death was a nice touch. Sheba and the kids and I carry out 'protest picnics', where we set up a picnic blanket ON RUNWAYS and tuck into our sandwiches (homemade slow-cooked bread with a lentil and organic turnip paste filling) right where the planes are supposed to be taking off! We have delayed seven flights in this fashion, which has at least lengthened the life of the planet for a couple of hours or so.

Jonty, avoid 'using force' against flying – that would only make you as bad as the unthinking holidaymakers. Instead, let us show them the terror of their ways through tough taxes, protest picnics and by sticking their names on a public register of shame.

 ## Is it ethical to own a car?

Dear Ethan,
In the 1990s, anti-roads protests were taking place
everywhere. Today, there are hardly any. Does this
mean roads are no longer an ethical issue? Because I
have to tell you Ethan, I was very sympathetic to the
anti-roads cause, but today I drive a Toyota Prius and
there is a new bypass being built round my way, which
will be very handy! Should I welcome this new road, or
re-grow my youthful dreadlocks, don my dungarees
and donkey jacket, and protest? It's OK to own a car
now, isn't it, Ethan? Come on!
James Whitelaw, Brighton, Sussex

Dear James,
First of all, please desist from using the phrase 'donkey jacket'; I know for a fact that donkeys find it demeaning. Second of all, do you remember nothing about the anti-roads protests?! Have you forgotten what was said on the placards we waved as we clashed with the Tarmac Terrorists and tried to prevent them from permanently

scarring Gaia's face with boiling black tar?! The placards said 'ROADS ARE RAPE' and 'MOTORWAYS ARE MURDER'. What part of 'RAPE' and 'MURDER' do you not understand?

You should be ashamed of yourself, James. Swampy – the Cromwell of the 1990s, that most brave warrior who went without soap or water for months in the name of saving the trees of Newbury from the Road Reich (and who was predictably labelled a 'soap-dodger' by the unthinking masses who are not mentally advanced enough to appreciate what he did for them) – will turn in his grave when he hears what you have asked me. (By 'grave' I mean 'political grave': Swampy, otherwise known as Daniel Hooper, is still alive, but such is the power of the Big Obese Corporate Monopoly Media that this leader of men and mortal threat to the status quo has been successfully sidelined, to the extent that nobody knows what has become of him.)

How quickly people forget why the anti-roads protests were so crucial! First, they helped to rout the road-builders and forever preserve sections of the 'countryside'. (ANOTHER word that I hate! 'Country' is a human concept and 'side' suggests that nature should be some-thing 'on the side', a nice green getaway for people who spend most of their lives in smoggy cities.) Second, the anti-roads protests helped to give birth to modern British environmentalism. Did you know that I, and many of the other eco-ethicists warning humanity about its carbon vomit-stain, were politically forged in the heat of the anti-roads revolution?

I turned green during the anti-roads uprising. First, green with anger at what the Road Rapists were doing to the trees of Newbury; then, green with envy at the searing intellect and implacable bravery of Swampy and his lieutenants (Shifty, Dogbreath and Y-front); and finally, green as in environmentalist, as in Righteous and True and Upstanding and Dignified. And I have remained that shade ever since.

Bliss was it in that dawn to be alive! The camaraderie! The sense of purpose! The sitting in trees for weeks on end with nothing but berries, nuts and leaves to furnish the linings of our stomachs! Our impassioned anti-tarmac chants shook the trees of Newbury, their leaves and twigs rustling in deep-felt appreciation for our selfless attempt to save them from the bulldozer that is humanity's one-eyed greed and destructiveness.

We brave few, we merry warriors . . . we did everything we could to save the forests from being plundered by road-builders. I and three others were charged with protecting one of the tallest, proudest oaks in Newbury. We lived in that tree for seven months, three weeks, four days, eight hours and twelve-and-a-half minutes. We adopted warrior names. Tarquin Alberwaithe from Oxford became 'Armpit'; Ernest Windsor-Montague from Hertfordshire became 'Mole'; Zachariah Devonshire from Edinburgh became 'Mudface'; and I, Ethan Greenhart from Kent, became 'Stinky'.

We handcuffed ourselves to the branches. When the planet-hating police removed our handcuffs on the trumped-up charge that they were 'dangerous weapons', we tied ourselves to the branches using our dreadlocks. When our dreadlocks snapped after being moistened by tree sap and rain (rain, what were you thinking?! We were on your side!), we clung on with our weakened arms and legs. And when our weakened arms and legs gave way, we fell one by one – first Mole, then Armpit, then Mudface, and finally, me, Stinky. We were so weak and malnourished, we didn't even have enough salt in our systems to shed a tear for our tree as it was abused and finally murdered by man-unkind. Thankfully, Zachariah's father sent one of his helicopters to pick us up, and we spent a few weeks recuperating at his castle in Scotland.

It was also during the anti-roads protests that I made my first ever appearance in the media . . . though not in circumstances of my choosing! When I fell from the tree and hit the ground, after months of clinging on for dear life (for the tree's dear life, that is, not my own), a gang of paparazzi circled me and started snapping. The following day, a photo of me was published in the *West Newbury Chronicle* under the headline 'NUT FALLS FROM TREE'. Mother and father were mortified. Both have positions of responsibility in local government in Kent, and it was quite trying for them to see their eldest son plastered across the front pages of various papers with broken dreadlocks hanging from his head and elderberries staining the sides of his mouth.

James, did we fight and starve and get humiliated by local news outlets for NOTHING? I'm sorry, but just because you ended up with a cushy life and a fancy, supposedly 'eco' car, that does not mean roads are suddenly OK and driving a car has become acceptable. Yes, it's true, as a ruthless climate-sceptic hack once revealed, that my love Sheba has a small car that she occasionally drives to local nuts and seeds stores . . . but you know what, James? I have never set foot inside Sheba's car. Not once. Occasionally, when we have to travel as a family over distances of five miles or so, I tag on to the back of the car with a rope and allow myself to be pulled along on a pair of non-metallic, non-plastic, eco-friendly roller-skates. This means I am naturally dragged along by the motion of the car without contributing to the CAUSE of that motion, and without breaking the group promise that Armpit, Mole, Mudface and I made ten years ago while huddling together for warmth in our Newbury tree: 'We hereby solemnly declare never to travel by any method other than foot or sustainably sourced coracle.'

Take a leaf from our book, James (hold on, what gives humans the right to 'take leaves'? See how our everyday language is stacked with human-centric, plantist phrases?): get rid of your Toyota Prius, put on those old dungarees, stop washing your hair, and go and protest against that bastard bypass.

☞ **Is it ethical to get into an ambulance?**

Dear Ethan,
I have a hypothetical question for you – or perhaps, a 'hypo-ethical' question! Would it be ethical to get into an ambulance in an emergency? The reason I ask is because, like you, I never travel by motorised vehicle.

But what if, Gaia forbid, I was involved in an accident? Would it be OK to enter an ambulance and be driven to a hospital?

Sean Adamson, Edinburgh

Dear Sean,

It may be a 'hypo-ethical' question for you, but it isn't for me. I have actually faced this very real, very dramatic dilemma. And I can confidently tell you: it is NOT ethical to get into an ambulance. Therefore, you must prepare an eco-alternative way of getting to a hospital in case of emergency.

Back in 2004, I was building a tree-house in our back garden, when a gust of wind swept me out of the tree and knocked me fifteen feet to the ground. I landed on my head, and was out cold. Sheba immediately called the emergency services. Well, not quite immediately. We don't have a phone on account of the fact that it is a ridiculously unnecessary use of electrical resources. We DO have an internet connection, but it is powered by an electricity generator connected to a treadle pump that is worked by our two children, and Sheba thought it would take too long to get the kids treadle-pumping and then to send an email to the local hospital asking them to send an ambulance. Of course our trusty carrier pigeon Beauty, who has so reliably delivered messages to our friends and family and who even carried my tax return to the Inland Revenue office in 2007, would be no good in this instance.

So Sheba ran to the nearby council estate – her bravery knows no bounds! – and asked a young girl if anybody in this unfortunate enclave owned a telephone or some other form of telecommunications device because we needed an ambulance at once. Lo and behold, even before Sheba had finished speaking, the girl herself had pulled out a flashing electronic gadget, apparently called a 'mobile phone', dialled 999 and demanded an ambulance for 'the cottage of weirdos who live next to the Steve Biko Estate'.

I have no recollection of what happened next, but apparently two paramedics put me on a stretcher and wheeled me into the ambulance. A few minutes later I woke up in my idea of hell . . . Sean, for the first time in *twelve years* I found myself *inside* a motorised, petrol-powered vehicle! When I woke I felt queasy and sore-headed as a result of the fall; when I realised where I was I just felt plain sick. My stomach turned; my head spun in time with the screeching siren; my hands became cold, clammy. I instantly demanded to be let out so that I could walk to the hospital. One of the paramedics said, 'The bang on his head was worse than we thought – he's hysterical,' until Sheba explained, 'Actually, he's always like this' – I'm sure she meant always ethical, always principled, always willing to harm himself if it protects Gaia from even a milligram of carbon. When my yelps of protest became too persistent for the paramedics to ignore, they let me out and, holding my handkerchief made from undyed, recycled sackcloth to my bloodied head, I nobly walked the last mile to the casualty department where I swiftly collapsed in an exhausted heap on a floor that smelt too much like chemically-based bleach for my liking.

This experience was such an eye-opener, Sean. I started an Ambulance Awareness campaign: I called on the Kent authorities to ensure that paramedics explicitly get a patient's consent BEFORE putting them in any kind of vehicle that burns petrol. This could be done by handing the injured party a consent form to sign, or by searching the injured party's pockets or wallet/purse to see if he/she is carrying an Ambulance Consent Card – a small card (made from recycled paper) that could be distributed by the government to those who are happy to board an ambulance. The local newspaper mocked my campaign. One of its oh-so-clever columnists made some point about how impractical it would be to get the seriously injured victim of a bombing or a train crash to sign an Ambulance Consent Form and asked if 'Mr Crankhart' (geddit?) would be happy to leave such non-consenting victims dying by the side of the road. In a letter to the paper I retorted: 'OK then, let's not bother asking patients for their consent, and instead ask Gaia whether she consents to allowing ambulances to speed, screech and skid across her pretty face.' Ha! 'Crankhart' 1, local newspaper 0.

What this shows, Sean, is that even those of us who live the pure and ethical life can be dragged kicking and screaming against our will into the messed-up modern world. If you get an injury, they stick you in a smog-coughing ambulance. If there's a fire at your home, they send a carbon-farting fire engine to sort it out. Fire engines are doubly problematic, of course, since they also use gallons and gallons of water to extinguish fires, as if humankind a) has the right to use water in such a violent fashion, and b) has any authority to put out fires which often only represent nature's fury with the plague of humans running riot on her person.

Sean, if you are serious about living a truly petrol-free life, then take a tip from the Greenharts. Since my horrifying experience waking up in an ambulance we have instituted our own eco-emergency services. We have constructed an emergency rickshaw – or a rick*sore* as we call it, given its injury-related function! It is made completely from bamboo, and Sheba, I and the kids have all carried out practice runs between our house and the A&E unit. Running at full speed and pulling a weight of 150lb, I can get there in eighteen minutes and six seconds; Sheba can do it in twenty-three minutes and thirteen seconds; the kids vary between thirty and thirty-five minutes. Ironically, on one of the practice runs, as my youngest boy pulled me on the ricksore, he suffered severe strains in his legs and arms – thankfully, we ended up in exactly the right place for him to have them treated . . .

Sean, find some ethical, non-ambulance reliant ways to deal with everyday emergencies, and then spend the rest of your time preaching to people about the all-consuming State of Global Emergency that shall shortly hospitalise us all.

☞ **Is it ethical to ride a bike?**

Dear Ethan,
I live in south London and travel into the city centre by bus every day. But I've had my fill of it! The buses

*are always late, always overcrowded, always full of
hooded youths playing tinny versions of gangsta rap
over the loudspeakers of their mobile phones. And
there is no way I would ever buy a car. So I have
decided to join the cycling revolution. But first I
wanted to check with the ethical oracle (that's you!): is
it OK to ride a bike?*

Shauna Lawler, Camberwell

Dear Shauna,
OK, first the good news about bikes: they are without
doubt more eco-friendly than cars. Now for the bad news:
riding a bike is not as ethical as you might think, and not
as eco-friendly as some of my naughty colleagues in the
world of ethical lifestyle advice have led people to believe.

Cyclists get a bad rap, so I don't want to be *too harsh*
on them. My good friend Emine, a keen cyclist, once
angrily told me about a 'comedy' sketch on a show
called *Monkey Dust* on BBC 3. It featured three stiff and
superior bike-riders whizzing through the streets of
London without a care or consideration for motorists
or pedestrians. Apparently they robotically intoned: 'We
are The Cyclists, the intermediate stage between humans
and pure energy, the most energy-efficient beings on the
planet. Everything we do is aimed at conserving the
earth's resources.' In one scene they ran over and killed a
dog and said to its owner: 'Do not worry, he is biodegradable.'

I asked Emine what she was getting so upset about: it
sounds to me like they presented cyclists in a *good* light. I

mean, it is MY main aim in life to become 'the intermediate stage between humans and pure energy' and to be
'the most energy-efficient being on the planet'. And while
of course I frown upon running over dogs, it is true that
they are biodegradable: ants, worms and other oppressed
creepy-crawlies can make a mighty feast of a deceased
dog.

People have a perception of cyclists as cocky and
arrogant. One newspaper columnist looked snottily down
her snout at the 'kamikaze, eco-warrior maniac with fixed
cycle gears who swears at children and has black elbows
from dipping them in fumes'. That's an insult?! What I
wouldn't give to be called a 'kamikaze, eco-warrior
maniac' – I want that on a badge, please! The columnist
continued: 'These politico-bikers are not actually interested in the business of getting anywhere: they're using the
bikes like sandwich boards, rather than vehicles.' If
ONLY cyclists were like that. In my experience, cyclists
are, if anything, too namby-pamby and overly interested
in getting from A to B rather than in using the entire
alphabet to string together some pro-bike, car-bashing
political slogans. A few years back, during my last college
term, I set up a pro-cycling group called the Two Wheel
Action Team (TWAT). Our aim was to extol the benefits
of two-wheeled transport over four-wheeled murder of
the planet, and to spread the word about the danger posed
by cars to people (accidents etc), the environment (smog
etc) and world peace (oil etc). Only two fellow students
signed up, and even they dropped out when I suggested
upping the ante and riding naked through Westminster

with slogans such as 'CARS CAUSE WARS' and 'TWAT FOREVER' daubed on our buttocks. Some people have no e-courage.

So, Shauna, if you take the cycling route, I hope you will be braver and more outspoken than most cyclists. Shout at those taxi drivers! Raise the middle finger to those truckers! Screw your face up in horror at obese pedestrians taking too long to cross the road because they have overeaten and under-exercised yet again! We need some real kamikaze, eco-warrior maniacs on the road, to put pressure on motorists and to prise apart the eyelids of the feckless populace so that they might see the truth about the damage cars and congestion are doing to Mother Earth.

But . . . there is a big fat but, Shauna. You need to be aware of a little-known but very important fact: bikes are bad for the environment, too. Seriously. Their rubber-tyred wheels are a product of humankind's crazed and insane dependence on oil. The Treehugger website reveals that 'all modern tyres and most inner tubes use butyl rubber' . . . and I hate to be the one to break this to you, Shauna, but butyl is a petroleum derivative. That's right, those who cycle are helping to sustain the oil industries, and thus war, and thus terrorism, and thus death and destruction, and thus very bad things in general. What a dilemma you face, Shauna! Stay on the CO_2-vomiting bus with its annoying (and whiffy, right?) passengers . . . or buy a bike and play a very small role – BUT STILL A ROLE – in the digging up and utilisation of Gaia's black bile. What's a girl to do?

Of course, it is entirely up to you. I would never presume to tell anyone what they should and should not do with their lives. But I will give you some friendly advice: don't buy a bike because if you do you are a stark staring hypocrite who moans about petrol-powered cars and yet rides a contraption with petrol-derived tyres. That is my position on cycling these days – I am now a Former Cyclist, a cyclist who has seen the light. Yes, it was painful to retire my trusty old bike, 'Monty', after the pair of us had travelled so far and wide together. Yes, my anti-bike stance has caused run-ins with cycling friends such as Emine, who two years ago threw a cup of herbal infused tangerine tea in my face after I said 'on yer bike' in a very sarcastic manner as she tried to convince me that cycling IS eco-friendly. But . . . if we are serious about weaning humankind off oil, and serious about living as ethically as is humanly possible, then the bicycles have got to go.

However, as I say, Shauna, it is down to you to make a completely free and informed choice: ride a bike and help to cause an unimaginably awful future of fiery carnage that will consume entire ecosystems and whole species of innocent beasts, or get back on the bus. You decide; no pressure.

 ## Is it ethical to walk?

Dear Ethan,
No, no, no, say it isn't true! Is walking bad for the environment?! A recent report says that walking can emit MORE carbon than driving. Can this possibly be

true, Ethan? And if it is, what should we do about it?
NEVER GO OUT AGAIN?

Yours, Confused of Chalmot

Dear Confused,
Oh dear, I was hoping none of my correspondents would raise this embarrassing issue: the little-known fact that even walking – that pleasant, ancient pastime enjoyed by everyone from the ethically attuned Neanderthals to the evil polluters of the Victorian era – has become a planet-wrecking activity! But I'm afraid it is true. In the ethical living world, walking is the last taboo; nobody wants to talk about it. But now I am going to unveil the shocking truth: WE MUST STOP WALKING.

Like you, Confused, I was disturbed when I read the reports in 2007 that said walking is bad for the environment. Chris Goodall, a leading Oxford-based Green Party activist, worked out that walking to the shops is worse for Gaia than driving to them. He based his study on the theory of 'beef miles'. He calculated that driving a typical British car for three miles adds around 0.9kg of CO_2 to the atmosphere. But if you walked the same distance you would burn 180 calories, and to replace those calories you would need around 100g of beef – the production of which would result in the release of 3.6kg of CO_2 into the atmosphere. In other words, on the basis of current food production and consumption practices, it is FOUR TIMES more harmful for Mother Nature if we walk to the shops than if we drive to them. As Goodall said, maybe the long-term solution is 'eating less and driving to save our energy'.

Goodall's report caused a great deal of upset among ethical walkers, I can tell you. I am a member of the Roundtable of Responsible Ramblers (RRR). We differ from all other ramblers in that we explicitly seek the earth's consent before we walk on it. We do this by standing naked for twenty-four hours in a field or on a patch of land on which we wish to ramble – if any of us develops a cold as a result, we take it as a sign that the earth is withholding its consent; but if we all get through it without so much as a sneeze or a sniffle, we take it as a green light from the green and pleasant land that we may tread on her with our eco-hiking boots (no spikes, no rubber soles). (PLEASE don't confuse us with those crazy naked ramblers who waddle *sans* clothes from John O'Groats to Land's End! We don't actually ramble in the nude, which would be completely insane!)

After Goodall's report was published, members of the RRR protested outside his offices in Oxford, and issued one of the shortest and sharpest press statements in the history of green campaigning: 'Walking is the safest and most eco-friendly form of transport, so there.'

Unfortunately, I felt I couldn't join my RRR comrades on this particular protest, because I believe Goodall has hit on a very basic fact about the human plague, which is this: we have industrialised the world and everything in it to such a terrible extent that even walking, that wonderfully free and easy pastime, is now powered by industry! Confused, I dread what I am about to write, but I MUST put it into words . . . we ourselves have become machines, driven by CO_2 as surely as if we were a car or a motorbike or an aeroplane.

Some friends of mine have said to me: 'A-ha, but not all of us eat beef! So that means the energy we use to walk is NOT a product of factory farming and thus NOT using up 3.6kg of CO_2 every three miles!' True, but even the pure and righteous food that we right-minded eco-lifers consume will be stained with some CO_2. Recently, over a lentil loaf and glasses of locally distilled, non-alcoholic beer, my good friend Rafe and I worked out our own Walking Emissions. I have a soft spot for lentils, as my readers will know . . . but what you don't know is that not ALL of my lentils are locally grown. Dear reader, I have been known to buy lentils that are flown from Canada (I am burning with shame as I write this . . .). Taking into account the CO_2 emitted in the production of these lentils, and in their transportation from Canada to Kent, I estimate that every mile I walk is powered by 0.9kg of CO_2! OH MY GOD, when I think of all the miles I've walked in my life . . . even I, Mr Ethical, am a ticking carbon cluster bomb.

Rafe came off even worse. He has a penchant for pineapples . . . special ones that are planted and cared for organically by a colony of free-range orang-utans in Bermuda. Factoring in the CO_2 produced in the construction of the orang-utans' sleeping quarters, the production of food and slop that keeps them alive, the electricity used by the machine that vacuum-packs the pineapples, the creation of the plastic packaging for the pineapples, and finally the transportation by air and road of the pineapples to the 'Organic Monkey Food' store on the outskirts of Kent, we worked out that every mile Rafe walks is powered by anywhere between 1.2 and 1.98kg of CO_2! Rafe was mortified. He even refused to walk from my kitchen table to his bike at the garden gate, complaining in a sobbing voice that if he did he would use '0.23g sodding kilograms of sodding CO_2!' Eventually I had to carry him to his bicycle, since my lentil-powered walk to the garden gate only uses 0.12g of CO_2.

I never thought I'd say this, Confused, but it seems it is more ethical to be a couch potato than an ethical walker! (By the way, I hate the poisonous insinuation in the phrase 'couch potato' that potatoes are lazy. In their self-production of starch and their sprouting of yellow and silvery flowers, they are actually far more active than most of the human 'couch potatoes' who spend all day watching *Loose Women* with one hand tucked into their trousers and the other fumbling in a jumbo-sized bag of Doritos.) Who knew that the slovenly classes who are glued to their couches, Jim Royle-style, are actually quite ethical?! If only they would turn off their power-guzzling TVs and stop eating junk food, they would be the perfect eco-citizens.

Like them, Confused, all responsible ethical lifers must walk as little as possible, at least until there has been a massive social and environmental shift in the way food is produced. It is not ethical to fly. It is not ethical to drive. It is not ethical to ride a bike. And it is not ethical to go for a walk. The essence of ethical living is in remaining perfectly still and immobile, and to that end, Confused, I shall be tying my legs together with rope made from ethical Manila hemp for the foreseeable future.

CARBON ABACUS

If you have ever flown overseas, add 100 beads. If you have ever taken a cheap flight overseas, add 1,000 beads.

If you own a car (that includes you, Sheba), add 100 beads. If you own a 4x4, add 200 beads. If you own a truck, van or caravan, add 300 beads.

If you have ever got into an ambulance, add ten beads if you were conscious while doing it, but only five beads if you were unconscious. Add no beads if you were dead.

If you ride a bike, add ten beads. If, however, you are a 'kamikaze, eco-warrior maniac with fixed cycle gears', take those ten beads away.

If you have ever gone for a walk, add ten beads. If you are a regular jogger, add twenty beads. If you are a regular rambler, but not a member of the Roundtable of Responsible Ramblers, add thirty beads.

Note your bead count here:

. . . .

6

ETHICAL POLITICS

Politics is a funny business. Not funny ha ha, but funny peculiar, hypocritical and downright Gaia-phobic.

These days, politicians of all persuasions claim to care about the environment, yet they continue to be chauffeured around in black Jags, flown to peace conferences in the Middle East, and taken on freebies to look at a polar bear floating on broken blocks of ice in the North Pole. Well, perhaps if you didn't take a smoggy return flight halfway around the world to gawp at the poor beast, Mr Politician, he'd have a bit more ice to play around with.

The truth is, politics is fundamentally unethical – not only because it's scandalous and stacked to the rafters with self-serving individuals who wouldn't know what a principle was if it jumped them in an alleyway, but also because the whole idea that humankind has a *right* to determine events is shot through with arrogance and avarice.

What about animals? And plant life? And the climate itself? Don't they get a say? History tells us that they do. Many a human civilisation has been brought down by big climatic shifts, its claims to superiority and dominance over nature exposed for the hot air that they are. And it seems the same will happen to us. What are a few million voters and a House or two of Parliament against the plague and pestilence that will be unleashed by a ferocious Mother Earth? Hell hath no fury like a Mother burned!

I also have a bit of a problem with democracy . . . not a popular view, I know, but then if I wanted to be popular I'd move to London and write about things like new hemlines and my favourite alcoholic tipple, instead of bravely raising the burning issues facing our burning planet. The problem with democracy is that it gives the biggest say to the biggest crowd – and I know from experience that it's hard to get through to big crowds! This means that I, devoted to the planet, supremely ethically aware and greener than the green, green grass of home, have the same amount of say in this country's direction as someone who works in a factory, say, or in a TV and hi-fi shop! How can that be right? It is brave souls like me who are drowned out by 'democracy'.

Read on to discover why politics is little more than a cover for humanity's continuing abuse of the mother of ALL parliaments: Gaia.

  Is it ethical to vote?

Dear Ethan,
I've been a fan of your weekly column for a long time.
But with all your profound advice on how we should
live our lives, it occurs to me that you've never
mentioned which political party you support, or even
whether you vote at all. Do you think that Labour, the

Tories, the Lib Dems or the Greens have the best policies? Who do you think I should vote for?
                                        Fran Chase, Manchester

Dear Fran,
There's an old anarchist slogan: 'It doesn't matter who you vote for, the government always gets in.' I would like to update that slogan: 'It doesn't matter who you vote for, *humans* always get in.'

I have actually stood in local council elections, and my experience confirmed my view of democracy as deeply unethical. Near our cottage in Kent, there was a small wooded area with some lying water, which had become home to a colony of rats. I have always had a fondness for rats, whose very life's work is to clear up after humans and try to make something useful out of our mountains of waste, and who occasionally keep overpopulation in check by charitably spreading diseases on Gaia's beleaguered behalf. However, the local council decided, in its infinite wisdom, to drain this patch of land so that an old people's home could be built upon it! Why on the face of Gaia would we want to destroy such a beautiful place, especially in the name of creating an institution for a bunch of resource-grasping wrinklies whose only purpose would be to generate more CO_2 as their Woodbine-polluted lungs thinly snatched for another desperate breath?

So I stood as an independent candidate and called myself the SOS Party (Save Our Swamp!). My arguments fell on the deaf ears of a dumb electorate. 'Why don't you fuck off, Swampy?' they would shout, foolishly confusing me with the legendary roads protester. When I spoke in the village square on why we should defend the ratty swamp, I was roundly booed. I even had a dead rat thrown at me, a lovely animal snatched from its resting place in the soil to become a weapon in some mindless thug's war against Nature and me, Nature's representative. I ended up mildly concussed; it was quite a large rat.

I soon realised that simply protecting the rats' swamp was no longer enough. In order to tackle the ignorance of voters, I decided it was time to launch a grander political vision. So, I unveiled my Manifesto Against Domination of Mother Earth and Nature (MADMEN) and stood in the General Election of 2005. I published a five-point plan on rice paper using soya-based ink. This meant that those who read my plan could afterwards eat it, digest it (literally as well as intellectually!), and then pass it through their anus and use the resultant excrement as compost on an allotment or in their garden. My five-point plan was:

1) The planet, not people, must come first. No tree, animal or insect should knowingly be sacrificed or injured in the name of benefiting humankind.
2) People must learn to conduct themselves within certain, planet-friendly limits and be harshly punished if they contravene the rules.
3) All scientific experimentation, especially animal experimentation, must be brought to an end. The teaching of science in schools – which perpetuates notions of human superiority – should be banned.

4) The production of books should be brought to an end. Not only do books, by their very existence, imply that humans are clever and important, they also use up too many resources in their production and transportation. However, book burning, while a good idea in principle, is too polluting to be considered.

5) People are generally slime – and we must be tough on slime, and tough on the causes of slime! The human population should be reduced by approximately 5.9 billion over the next 100 years.

I roped Sheba in to help me distribute my rice-paper plan to the people of Kent (some of whom ate it *before* reading it, the philistines!). I employed my two kids as canvassers and we went from door to door asking people, 'What's more important: the survival of planet Earth or your pointless two-week holiday in Riga?' I challenged my fellow candidates to live debates about the big issues facing Kent/the universe. A Lib Dem and a representative of the Monster Raving Loony Party took part in a soap-box debate with me in the village square. We discussed everything from making recycling compulsory by royal edict (my idea) to whether police officers should wear luminous yellow polka dot pillbox hats instead of black helmets (the Monster Raving Loon's idea). And since a TV news crew was present, I took the opportunity to launch the *rap version* of my five-point plan, which I thought would help to attract the all-important youth vote. I raised my megaphone and hip-hopped at the top of my lungs:

The planet comes first, people are the worst,
We really must live within our limits!
We don't need to test 'cos Nature knows best,
You can take all human knowledge and bin it!
People are slime – you know wot, being human
  is a crime! Yo.

Fran, this manifesto-as-ditty really could have opened young voters' eyes to the problem of unethical living, but . . . I was made a fool out of by the evil, environment-baiting, lie-happy, corrupt, cowardly, corporate media. The TV station aired sections of my song alongside the Monster Raving Loony guy talking about making naked unicycle-riding compulsory, in an item headlined 'Respectable Lib Dem Involved in Shouting Match with Two Extremists'. Guess how many votes I got in the General Election after that? Twelve! And eight of them were from Sheba, Sheba's mum and dad, and our friends Zac, Margo, Emine, Rafe and Jonty. The other four, I discovered later, came from a local mental health facility, which relaxed its rules in 2005 in order to allow inmates to vote.

I decided to give up on politics, and you should too. Concepts of 'the majority' are only an excuse for the rule of the TV-intoxicated mass that cares little for the planet over the far smaller number of us who know in our hearts that Gaia faces a dire future. Yet Nature still needs her representatives . . . now more than ever. So I will continue to think up new ways in which I might represent her interests outside of the hellish electoral process. My name is Ethan Greenhart, and I am ready to answer the call of nature.

Is it ethical for the government to prevent floods?

Dear Ethan,
I live on the outskirts of Witney, which has been hit by quite a few floods in recent years. My neighbours and I watched with horror as the floodwaters rose in summer 2007 . . . and then we watched in horror as various man-made, and probably quite unethical, efforts were made to stop the flooding. What is the most ethical way for the authorities to prevent floods?

Jemima Routledge, Witney

Dear Jemima,
Yes, the floods that have rocked England of late have indeed been tragic. At times, I have hardly been able to watch the evening news through our next-door neighbour's living room window (we Greenharts have no TV, of course): all that awful, heart-wrenching footage of water naturally breaking its banks, like tears of rage bursting forth, only to find its watery path blocked by brick homes, shops, cars, groups of 'residents', and journalists in wellies (who no doubt poison the water with their serpent-like TV camera cables, the rubber on their boots, and the Gaia-phobic bile that passes for on-the-ground reporting these days).

If it isn't bad enough that we caused the earth to weep in this manner in the first place – with our ceaseless carbon-mongering which has unquestionably given rise to more freaky weather – now we have the blind arrogance to stand in the way of these floods of anger, to try to stop them, to ask: how can we prevent such a thing from happening again?! I have a different question to yours, Jemima – not 'what is the most ethical way to prevent floods' but 'who are *we* to prevent them at all?'

You ask what my flood advice is? To leave the rivers alone. To let them burst and run free and wash away the grotesque footprint that has been left by farmers, factories and 'residents', just as the sea washes away prints left in the sand by flip-flop-wearing holidaymakers/planet-destroyers. (By the way, I am continually horrified by the audacity of people who call themselves 'residents', as if they OWN the land. You are guests here, not 'residents'! On the other hand, my *Oxford English Dictionary* reveals that the word 'residence' can also mean 'that which settles as a deposit; the residuum or deposit left after any chemical process'. Now *that* sounds like a good description of these gangs of humans who set up chemicalised and smog-producing camps – otherwise known as 'local communities' – in areas of natural beauty where rivers run wild.)

Let's not beat around the bush here, Jemima: the recent floods are of man's making. We have prodded and cajoled the environment, mocked it and muddied it, and then we're surprised when it fights back! What do we expect? If you ask me, these floods are the natural equivalent of when some black-clad kid who listens to Marilyn Manson and gets bullied by the jocks and the cheerleaders goes on a school shooting spree – after all, if you push someone or some*thing* too far, guess what: it breaks.

Some people have asked: where is the proof that the floods in England over the past couple of years are a product of global warming? In the *Daily Mail* (eeeurrghhh!) the once-respectable BBC weatherman John Kettley wrote of the floods in Witney in July 2007: 'In my view, none of the [recent] severe weather we have experienced is proof of "climate change". It is just a poor summer – nothing more, nothing less – something that was the norm throughout most of the Sixties.' I cannot believe that people like this – DENIERS – still have jobs. Note how he puts 'climate change' in quote marks! How grotesque! Imagine someone putting the Nazis' 'genocide' in quote marks. In my personal-political view, having the likes of Kettley working in the area of weather is like putting David Irving in charge of a Holocaust Museum (or perhaps 'Holocaust' Museum) or allowing Rose West to run a halfway house for young runaways.

So they want proof that these watery uprisings are a response to our rape of nature, do they? Tell me this: what is proof? I don't mean to come over all Pontius Pilate (a man I detest for his destruction of trees in the name of making crosses; I wince for nature every time I see a brainwashed Christian wearing a crucifix around his or her neck), but Pilate did have a point: *what is truth*? Proof is an arrogant human concept, beloved of oil-funded scientists and twisted politicians. I shall not play their disgusting game. Suffice to say, I know and you know and *Nature knows* that the recent floods are the first stirrings of a climate catastrophe to come. We can simply feel it in our waters. So to speak.

And you know what? On this basis we should welcome floods rather than try to prevent them. I'm with Jeremy Leggett, a former adviser to the New Labour government no less, who said the floods of 2007 were 'bills' from God, who is lurking behind the 'gathering clouds' and frowning down on polluting humanity.

More than that, I'm with the *Guardian* columnist Madeleine Bunting who, in 2000, during a previous outbreak of nature's weeping, effectively said 'bring it on!' 'Apathetic about climate change and out of touch with the environment, Britain needs a short sharp shock,' said Bunting. 'The best chance Britain has is a course of environmental ECT: lots of small, nasty shocks where it really hurts. So roll on [floods], they've got a lot to teach us. The more floods, the merrier.'

Yes! Let the floodwaters rise, and the nastier and more shocking their consequences, the better. That'll teach us to build towns and villages in green spaces, to drive cars and take holidays, to think ourselves above nature. My goodness, Jemima, how kind nature is! Her floods are not horrible – rather, they are a selfless lesson for humanity about its disgusting behaviour and a polite-but-firm warning to us to change our ways. That nature can be so kind as to give us clear warnings, even after EVERYTHING we've done to her, is enough to make me weep floods of tears, too.

Is it ethical to be a Tory?

Dear Ethan,
I have always hated the Tories since that witch
Thatcher snatched the milk from the nation's
schoolchildren, sacked all the miners and more or less
destroyed the entire country in the Eighties. But now I
see that David Cameron says we should vote blue to
go green, and what's more they have employed the eco-
superstar Zac Goldsmith to educate us all about ethical
living. I'm confused! Can we greens be on the same
side as super-rich snobs like Goldsmith?

Dave, Hackney

Dear Dave,
Let's get this straight from the start. The environment
belongs to no man – or even woman. The planet is not a
political football. Like all true eco-warriors, I believe that
it is far too important to be polluted by politics. And like
all right-minded folk, I hate football anyway.

It's not what plastic party badge you wear on your
chest that matters; it's what is in the heart that you wear
on your organic hemp sleeve that counts. Was it ethical
to be in the Nazi Party? Probably not. Actually, it
definitely wasn't, now I come to think about it. But
could somebody who called themselves a Nazi still hold
ethical beliefs? No doubt. Even Hitler was a vegetarian,
an animal rightist, an organic farming man *and* an anti-
smoker! Whereas that Himmler was a chicken farmer –
the fascist!

143

So let's not be blinded by corporate brands like 'Tory'. And while we are de-junking our minds, Dave, you might want to challenge some of your more macho assumptions about Margaret Thatcher's government. It turns out that she did our kids a favour in banishing all that free milk from schools: we now know just how much damage that product of the toxic dairy industry was doing to their young bodies. As the MilkSucks website puts it, 'Milk Sucks . . . for animals, for the environment and for your health!' As for Thatcher closing down the British coal mines – well, such a blow against the evil fossil fuel industry might well have extended the life of the entire planet for around a fortnight. What are a few thousand miners' livelihoods when set against that victory for Gaia?

Actually, Dave, lots of Conservatives have always been big on conservation – the clue is in the name, it seems. So let's try to look at the party and its claims to be green without the political blinkers. Consider its green-leaning 'Quality of Life' report, written by Zac Goldsmith and John Gummer and published in 2007. That report represented the most brilliantly justifiable waste of paper resources of recent years. It proposed getting rid of white lines in the middle of the roads, a genius move that would make most roads all but impassable thanks to wrecked cars, forcing people to find other ways to travel. And it suggested switching off all street lights: an EXCELLENT idea that would keep petrified citizens indoors instead of going out bingeing on booze and carbon.

You see, Dave, your prejudices about 'greedy' Tories are *so* last decade – they have embraced the spirit of self-sacrifice and austerity. Indeed, the 'Quality of Life' report even contained a lengthy chapter entitled 'The Darker Side of Wealth'. Of course, what else should we expect from my favourite green genius, and pretty close friend, Zac G? He does not understand these things in spite of his personal wealth, but BECAUSE of it. Who better to see through our addiction to wealth than the Man Who Has Everything? His inherited fortune of millions (and millions!) means that he can rise above grubby consumerism and see the damage it is doing. If only the credit-sucking working classes, who scrimp and save and then spend their money on burp-producing alcopops and Chum for their dangerous dogs, could see things as clearly as Zac does.

Avert your inverted snobbery, Dave, and you'll see that many of the best green thinkers come from so-called 'posh' backgrounds. Peter Melchett, former head of Greenpeace and now policy director for The Soil Association, is a baron and the Eton-educated son of Sir Julian Mond, former chairman of the British Steel Corporation. Jonathon Porritt, chair of the government's Sustainable Development Commission, is another Eton graduate and the son of Lord Porritt, the eleventh Governor General of New Zealand. Then there's the Optimum Population Trust (OPT), one of my favourite organisations, which campaigns TIRELESSLY to reduce the number of people living on the planet by describing having large families as an 'eco-crime' and pointing out how terrible it is that so many black babies are being born in Africa (not on race lines, silly, but because they are adding to the plague on the planet that is rampant humanity). The OPT has among its patrons the aforementioned Porritt, as well as Sir Crispin Tickell and the actress Susan Hampshire, who also goes by the name Lady Kulukundis since she married a knighted Greek shipping magnate.

Then, of course, there's Prince Charles – Bonnie Prince Charlie, the green prince and heir not only to the throne of England but to the throne of my heart for his brave championing of sustainable development, his organic all-butter shortbread biscuits, and for having in-depth conversations with gladioli. There's also my new hero David de Rothschild, who wrote the brilliant *Live Earth Global Warming Survival Handbook*, a lovely, cartoon-packed tome which contains intelligent tips for simple, meek, eco-friendly living. No doubt it was David's supremely privileged upbringing – he's a mem-ber of the mind-blowingly wealthy Rothschild banking family and an heir to its fortune – that led him to see the light about 'the dark side of wealth'. What courage it takes to use your wealth to tell others that living like an eco-pauper – poor in crappy materialist goods but rich beyond your wildest dreams in feel-good eco-moralism – is the most ethical state of being on today's warming planet.

Dave, we need brave men and women to take a lead and *convince* the blob (sorry, but what else can we call it?) to change its ways. And if those men and women come from feudalistic backgrounds, where a passionate love for the countryside has always rubbed shoulders with a readiness to punish people who want more, more, more, then that's all the better. Zac, Charles, Jonathon, David – lead us from this hell we have created!

Is it ethical to boycott Japan?

Dear Ethan,
I am so furious with the Japanese for continuing to hunt whales! It makes me want to scream! But I want to do something more useful than that . . . Tell me, would it be ethical to boycott everything Japanese – all of their food, electrical products, and so on? I think that would hit Japan where it really hurts and make them rethink their bloody expeditions in the Antarctic.
Sheila Mayweather, Dorset

Dear Sheila,
If I had a penny for every tear I've shed over Japan's mad massacre of these great big majestic cows of the ocean, I'd have at least £2.89. We are witnessing nothing less than whaleocide: illegal butchery of one of Gaia's proudest, most intelligent and peaceful beasts by one of Gaia's cruellest, most callous and war-thirsty peoples: the Japanese.

Sorry if that offends my sensitive readers, or indeed my Japanese readers. But then, you people have no idea what it's like to have a metal stake fired into your back at 100mph, do you? (If you *have* had an experience along those lines, please let me know: every year I collate an audio/visual/touch/feel/smell exhibition for our local church hall called 'When Whales Weep'.) Whales MUST be defended! It is a scientifically proven fact that whales share 97.4 per cent of their genes in common with humans and have an IQ level higher than the average owner of a pit-bull terrier. Whales kept in captivity have also been trained to develop an appreciation for Radio 4 comedy and to recognise the difference between a plate of guacamole and a plate of mushy peas. How can we kill these Einsteins of the animal world?

My mother – a Middle-England, helmet-hair type, whose own father was on the receiving end of Japanese cruelty during the Second World War (which means my family has real and direct empathy with what the whales are experiencing) – used to say: 'Oooh, the Japanese are a cruel race.' I would get so embarrassed. 'Don't be backward!' I'd tell her. Now it seems Mum might have been right all along: what more evidence do we need of Japan's innate cruelty than its bloodying of the Antarctic Ocean with the guts and innards of entire communities of minke and humpback, and probably some dolphins too while they're at it?

Let's not beat around the bush here. As one Australian columnist said, the Japanese are indulging in 'uncivilised barbarity', and the Australian government must send a clear 'message to Tokyo': 'This is the last time your barbarity will be tolerated.' Yes! Other commentators have described the Japanese as 'terrorists' (actually, when did al-Qaeda ever use harpoons against man or beast?), and as 'viciously cruel' (Mum, I hope you're reading this – vindicated at last!).

Easily the best thing to come out of this horrific massacre of unsuspecting daddy, mummy and baby whales is that Australia is FINALLY taking seriously its role as the guardian of animal rights in that rather reckless corner of the world, the Pacific. Many Oriental and Polynesian cultures have a shockingly backward attitude to animal well-being and self-esteem. Some of them even eat dogs! And ducks! I was horrified to my very core when I walked through Chinatown in Leicester Square recently and saw skinned, scorched and sautéed ducks hanging from hooks in the windows of Chinese slaughterhouses (some people call them 'restaurants'). I wrote a stern letter to the Mayor of London asking why he had allowed such a horrendous, alien culture to be imported into the capital city of the most animal-loving nation on Gaia's good earth, and what did I get for my troubles? A verbal warning from an official at the Commission for Racial Equality.

Yes, we should congratulate the Aussie government for decreeing that the Japanese whale hunt is illegal. And I was super-delighted to see that a letter spelling out Australia's case against Japan was hand-delivered to the Japanese whaling fleet in early 2008 by two radical anti-whaling activists from a ship that had been trailing and wailing at the evil whalers for months! The activists leapt on board the whalers' vessel of rotting flesh and murderous stench and handed the bamboozled, blood-stained harpooners a letter containing a stern telling-off from Aussie PM Kevin Rudd. What a wonderful act of unity this was, Sheila, between a sensible government keen to police its neighbours' stab-happy barbarism and radical activists who recognise no border or limit in their effort to save the whale/the planet/the deluded people of the Pacific from their own stupidity.

I like to think that the Aussies are anti-whaling because they are imbued with good ol' British values. All of those British convicts shipped to Australia in centuries gone by brought one useful thing with them: a very English love for animals! Now, Sheila, we must call on *other* level-headed, British- and European-influenced governments in less than level-headed parts of the world to follow Australia's lead and take action against anti-animal savagery.

For example, we should pressure the authorities in South Africa, which have strong European influences, to do something about elephant slaughter in Botswana. The local government of the Falkland Islands ought to challenge Argentina's mistreatment of dogs (there are *millions* of strays, apparently). And perhaps the people on the rock of Gibraltar can cross over into Spain proper and do something, ANYTHING, about Spaniards' harassment and stabbing to death of bulls and their grotesque abuse and starvation of donkeys. Around the world, responsible animal-loving nations must wage war (er, metaphorically, not literally) against reckless, irresponsible, dog-eating nations. Some people say this is xenophobic, that animal rights campaigners – always defending donkeys from Spaniards, bears from Russians and whales from the Japanese – are imbued with fear and loathing for Johnny Foreigner. NO! We don't hate foreign people! We hate *all* people.

So yes, Sheila, by all means boycott EVERYTHING that says 'Made in Japan' on it. But you must also go further if you want to save the whales. You must also join my daily protest outside the Japanese Embassy in London (chants include, 'Whalers, do the world a favour: commit hara-kari'); write letters to every Japanese person you know (they must bear *collective responsibility* for their government's slaughter); and then consider helping me to finish building my own boat, *The Enola Gay*, which I hope to launch soon, with the aim of finding and foul-mouthing those evil whalers in the bloodied Antarctic.

 ## Is it ethical to censor climate change deniers?

Dear Ethan,
Everywhere I look, I seem to see people DENYING climate change. Spokesmen for the oil industry, right-wing newspaper columnists, supposedly edgy documentary filmmakers . . . they are all spreading the poisonous message that the planet isn't getting much hotter, or that if it is getting hotter it isn't humankind's fault. What should be done about such dangerous propaganda? Is it ethical to demand censorship of climate change deniers?
Tiggy Sherbourne, Hampshire

Dear Tiggy,
Not only is it ethical to demand censorship of climate change deniers, it is essential. These hideous denials of global warming do not only cast doubt on the indisputable and implacable scientific truth that unless we reduce our

carbon emissions by 92.8 per cent within the next eight years, seven months and two weeks the planet will be consumed by a hellfire so furious it will make the Book of Revelation look like a *Famous Five* novel – they also *contribute* to the further burning of future generations in a Hot Weather Holocaust by giving permission to the wide-eyed populace to indulge their craven instincts on the basis that there's nothing to worry about. With just a few poisonous words or doctored graphs, these deniers are helping to take YEARS off the life of our planet. Ban them? They should be glad we aren't charging them with aiding and abetting Grimes Against Humanity.

TV executives, newspaper editors and media moguls in general should know better than to publish or broadcast DENIAL. These are educated and civilised people. I mean, some of them ride bicycles, for goodness sake! They read the *Guardian*, shop at Waitrose, and watch European films with subtitles. In short, Tiggy, they're a lot like you and me, and they have a RESPONSIBILITY to protect the more slovenly and Pavlovian sections of British society from misinformation about global warming. Every time a denier slips on to the airwaves or into newsprint, it is because the upper echelons of the culturati have failed miserably in their duty to Mother the Nation (or perhaps Chaperone the Chavs!) and shield our eyes from lies.

So yes, censor the deniers, NOW. There are various ways we can do this. First, there is the *personal method* – make sure that all forms of climate change denial are expunged from your own and your family's everyday lives. The Greenhart household, for example, has completely shut itself off from anyone who denies, doubts or questions the truth about man-made climate change. We enforce this by making everyone who visits our home – from the children's friends right through to the local vicar – take a written test. We ask them questions such as 'Do you agree with Chapter 2, Verse 3 of the gospel according to the Intergovernmental Panel on Climate Change, which says we have but ten years to reduce world-wide carbon emissions by 60 per cent or else face fiery doom?', and 'What is your attitude to Al Gore's assertion in his film *An Inconvenient Truth* that there will be a sea-level rise of 20 feet in the near future following the melting of ice of West Antarctica?' Only those who score over 80 per cent are allowed into our home. Those who score between 80 and 90 per cent are given 'speaking rights' in *chez* Greenhart – that is, they are permitted to engage in conversation with me, Sheba and the kids. Those who score more impressively, between 90 and 100 per cent, are given speaking, hugging and eating rights, allowing them to share more fully in the Greenhart experience. This force-field of truth helps to protect our children and our homely ethos from the polluting words of doubters, deniers and 'debaters' (people who want to 'debate' global warming – how absurd!).

Sheba is not *entirely* happy with the current set-up. Because her father foolishly questions certain aspects of Al Gore's film, he continues to fail our truth test and has not been able to step over the Greenhart threshold for more than eighteen months. We do, however, allow him to watch our extended family get-togethers through the kitchen window, and to tap the kids on the head over the garden gate – he does *not*, however, have either speaking rights or hugging rights with the children.

Second, there is the *political method* of dealing with denial. We must put pressure on our leaders to extinguish all expressions of denial from public life. We should set up a House of Unscientific Activities and every individual who works in the public sphere should be made to swear: 'I am not now, nor have I ever been, a denier, doubter or debater of global warming.' That should sort the wheat from the chaff. (Another human-centric phrase I hate! Who are we to separate wheat from chaff, or to judge chaff so harshly? Come to think of it, what is chaff?)

Third, Tiggy, there is the *legal method* for combating denial: put deniers on trial for their wicked words. My fellow eco-adviser Mark Lynas has bravely called for 'future international criminal tribunals' for those who 'preach the gospel of denial' and who will be 'partially but directly responsible for millions of deaths from starvation, famine and disease in the years ahead'. Yes! If the deniers do not desist from their evil antics, we should set up an eco-Nuremberg that will hand out stiff sentences to any-one who has abused their 'right to speak' by speaking the untruth about climate change. (Sheba's dad had better watch out.)

Yet I wonder, Tiggy, if even this goes far enough? Perhaps deniers should not be tried, but *sectioned* under mental health legislation? Is it time we labelled climate change denial a mental disorder, and called on the American Psychiatric Association and other bodies to recognise it as such? After all, the scientific evidence is so over-whelmingly, unquestionably, unbelievably, supremely and insanely airtight that anyone who questions it must surely be . . . off his trolley, or so addicted to oil and other fossil fuels that his ability to think clearly and speak sensibly has been irrevocably and fatally compromised. If the personal, political and legal methods to combat denial don't work, Tiggy, I think we should keep in store one final option: mental health treatment for persistent deniers, and *eco-lobotomies* for really persistent deniers. Only then, through the final removal of warped brain matter, can we be truly confident that our life-and-death message about saving the planet is not being diluted by evil men and women.

CARBON ABACUS

If you have ever voted, add ten beads. If your vote was for the Green Party you may take away eight of those beads (the two remaining beads are for using a wood-pulped ballot paper).

If you have ever been involved in an effort to prevent flooding, add twenty beads. If you are engaged in long-term research to prevent floods, re-point storms or in some other way 'eco-engineer' the atmosphere to make it more comfortable for human beings, add 500 beads.

If you are a Tory, add five beads. If you are a Tory who is friendly with Zac Goldsmith, take those five beads away. If you are an aristocrat who hunts foxes, add 500 beads. If you are an aristocrat who heads up a green organisation and makes numerous media appearances telling people to change their behaviour and save the planet, add no beads. Have some port instead and pat yourself on the back.

If you have ever bought a Japanese boy, t-shirt, Hello Kitty lunchbox or electrical device, add fifty beads. If you have ever eaten whale meat, add 4,000 beads. If you have ever hunted whales, there are not enough trees on our planet or on all the possible life-sustaining planets in the entire universe combined to produce enough beads to measure your moral turpitude.

If you are a climate change denier, take the carbon abacus and shove it where the sun – which is NOT the cause of global warming, thank you very much – does not shine.

Note your bead count here:

. . . .

7

ETHICAL ENTERTAINMENT

For some bizarre reason, ethical lifestylists like me have won a reputation for being curmudgeonly. But we are not anti-joy. It's just that we think there is a time and a place for 'fun'. And the time is *not* 2008, and the place is *not* a planet that we have overheated like some strawberry-flavoured pop tart.

'Fun' is a human construct, and like most human constructs it is packed full of glaring contradictions. We shouldn't forget that what seems like 'fun' for human-kind is pure hell for other living creatures, both sensate and insensate.

When children throw sticks and stones into conker trees to knock down some nuts, do they ever think how the tree might feel? More to the point, when they drill a hole into the conker, and then freeze it for forty-eight hours and coat it in varnish to make it tougher, before smashing it at full speed against another similarly abused conker, do they ever stop to think how the conkers might feel? Of course they don't, because they are encouraged to 'have fun' without thinking about the consequences.

If we are serious about living more ethically, then we must strike a balance between fun and responsibilities.

We've had 'safe sex' (well I haven't – see my earlier stated opposition to condoms), and now we must institutionalise the idea of 'safe fun'. Entertainment is a very important part of human life, but it must be ethically aware entertainment. It must not come at the expense of the planet, or otherwise we're no better than those Neanderthals (with apologies to Neanderthal man) who allow themselves to be 'entertained' by bear-baiting, fox-hunting, slug racing, and all the other sick sports humankind has conjured up for larks.

Did you know that 'fun' comes from the archaic word 'fond', which means 'to befool'? It's quite fitting, since in having so much fun humankind is 'befooling' itself – befooling itself into believing that everything is hilarious and hunky-dory when in fact we have about ten years left to save the planet from floods, hurricanes, plagues, pestilence and probably swarms of locusts to boot.

Laughter and entertainment risk distracting us from the far more urgent task of living as quietly and meekly as possible in order to stop angering the gods of the natural world. Plus, I am pretty convinced that laughing out loud emits more noxious gases than just smiling and speaking normally. Is it being a killjoy to tell people to stop having joy while killing the world? If so, I'm a serial joy-killer, and proud of it!

Dig into this chapter to learn some tips about bad fun (football, TV, general merriment) and good fun (lentil-loaf get-togethers, planting seeds, watching dolphins).

Is it ethical to watch sport?

Dear Ethan,
With football, rugby and cricket and even motor racing
becoming more and more popular, I am confused as to
what I ought to think about sport. On the one hand,
playing sport is healthy, especially for children. On the
other hand, there seems something off about the dog-
eat-dog laddishness of a lot of sport, not to mention all
the money-mad consumerism now spoiling it. So Ethan,
is it possible to be an ethical sports fan?

Jonny, Rugby

Dear Jonny,
You like healthy sport? Well then, why don't you get a few
pals together, with some guns and knives and clubs and
whatnot, and go out trampling across the countryside in
the fresh air hunting foxes or deer or puppies? You'll all
have a marvellous time, get a healthy rosy glow (both
from the warm blood inside your cheeks and the hot blood
of your victims splattered across your faces), and you can
simultaneously work up an appetite and kill something to
eat.

You want sport that can bring people together and
make them feel good? Why not get a toothless old bear,
chain it to a pole (preferably made out of some rare and
irreplaceable tree), then poke it with sharp sticks and
kitchen implements before you bring on the specially
starved dogs to tear the bear to pieces (and if you're lucky
the bear will rip a few of them apart as well)? In my

159

experience, that should get all the people – and especially the children – laughing and enjoying themselves together like nobody's business.

Of course, readers, I am using irony and sarcasm here to make my point in a clever way. Do Not Try This At Home.

But, I hear you object, those are nasty old blood sports, not our nice modern consumer-friendly sporting occasions. Ha! *All* sports are blood sports. Whichever of your favoured little boys' games you might be indulging in, I'm afraid that the planet and biodiversity are the losers, and human aggression, avarice and vulgarity are the winners.

Football, rugby and the like? Organised violence, a way of socialising young boys to believe that beating, thrashing, crushing, mauling, kicking or hammering is not only natural and within the rules, but a good thing. These sports brainwash boys to accept notions of racial, sexual and even species-based superiority, and teach them that it is a jolly good jape to persecute a more sensitive boy (I won't mention any names) who might have been interested in loving the earth beneath his feet rather than trampling it to death.

The Olympic spirit? About as palatable as methylated spirit. An insane celebration of human hubris, popularising the arrogant idea that men can be like gods sitting up on Mount Olympus, rather than scum in the gutter of the earth. This 'spirit' is the epitome of a sporting ethos that absurdly suggests some people are 'better' than others because they can go faster, higher or further, rather than because, just say, they are more conscientious about recycling their household waste. When the Olympic horror show comes to London in 2012, I shall make sure I am deep in the rainforest.

That is before we even get on to considering all the pigs' bladders torn bloody and weeping from their little piggie tummies to make footballs, and all of the cat gut ripped screaming from helpless felines to make tennis racquets. 'Tiger' Tim? Cat-stranglers the lot of them, more like.

The clearest expression of the Neanderthal brutishness of competitive sport is, of course, boxing. Here we see man in all his gory 'glory', the thin veneer of civilisation ripped asunder along with the facial tissue to reveal not the 'beast within' but the bloody essence of humanity. (Which reminds me, Jonny, please don't let me hear you use the speciesist phrase 'dog-eat-dog' again – it's a man-eat-all-animals world we live in.) Still, at least boxing has the advantage that a decent number of the participants end up so brain-damaged that they will no longer be a threat to anything except the health service budget.

As for your mention of motor sport, words fail me. Racing cars, burning fossil fuels, rubber and the rest of it, for pleasure?! Formula One – more like Formula Wanton! A bunch of Grand Pricks, indeed. Frankly, you might as well hold a competition to see who can blow up the planet first – just for laughs.

However, Jonny, if there is one thing more despicably unethical than playing sports, it is watching them. What excuse could there be for spectating, aka inciting others to behave so disgracefully? Where competitive sports bring out the worst in the human individual, spectator sports bring together something far worse – the Human Crowd, the mob, the actual embodiment of humanity's biblical plague upon the planet.

Individuals are bad enough and do enough damage on their own, but a crowd is far worse than the sum of its parts. It is a beast – no, that would be a good thing! – correction, it is a monster such as nature could never conceive. I challenge anybody who seriously believes that democracy – the dictatorship of the ignorant carbon-bingeing consumers over the enlightened few – can be a 'good thing' to go within a mile of a football match (I do not suggest getting any closer if you value your life), and just glimpse the truth about the chip-fat-caked, lager-soaked seething mob wearing its colours of hate on its smoking-related-cancer-ridden chest with pride.

Then there's the small matter of the way that a brain-frying obsession with watching hairy men chase balls and each other around is distracting billions of people from facing up to the reality of the eco-crisis that is staring back at all of us from the eco-mirror. Basically, if it was not for football, it is obvious that world leaders would have accepted my message by now.

Apparently, some reactionary old football manager once suggested that this so-called sport was more impor-tant than mere life and death. It is time to accept that he was right, inasmuch as the blood sport of the crowd has itself become a matter of life and death for the entire planet – a planet that they treat as a ball to be kicked around. Somebody else once observed that the Puritans wanted to ban bear-baiting not so much because of the suffering of the bear but because of the pleasure the crowd got from watching it. He said that as a criticism . . . I say, three cheers for the Puritans! Restraining the mob's bloody 'pleasures' is our only hope of saving all the bears and the rest of biodiversity.

So Jonny, be strong, stand tall and Just Say No to sport. And if you still want something constructive, healthy and fun to do at the weekend, you could join one of my regular sponsored meditations in support of the 'Kick Sport Out of Schools!' campaign.

 ## Is it ethical to own a TV?

Dear Ethan,
Look, it is all very well living the eco-life, which I do.
But we need some joy in our lives, too! I desperately
want to buy a television set so that I can while away
the hours watching interesting documentaries, and so
that I will know what the hell people at work are
talking about when they say Desperate Housewives *or*
'Trevor McDonald'. So, Ethan, I'm going to get a TV,
OK?

Esther Madely-Sumner, St Albans

Dear Esther,
That's fine, go ahead. Mother Earth will understand, I'm sure. Never mind the fact that in buying a TV you are purchasing a toxic bomb packed with poisonous chemicals and helping to sustain the consumerist-catastrophist dictatorship that is modern capitalism. No, just so long as

you can watch some mad American soap about mad American housewives while sitting there in your (probably silk) pyjamas munching on cookies and cream ice-cream made from the kidnapped juices of penned-in cows . . . that's all that really matters, right, Esther?

How selfish can you get! And you claim to live the eco-life?! Well, I've got news for you, missy – after throwing a rare white tiger off a cliff and starting a forest fire in California, buying a TV is the third most environmentally unfriendly thing a human being can do.

There are two fundamental problems with television sets. First there is what is INSIDE them (horrible toxins), and then there is what comes OUT of them (vile human-centric nonsense and lots of adverts for unnecessary consumer goods mostly made in China and flown here by aeroplane). In other words, not only are TVs made from a variety of disgusting chemicals – they also trigger a variety of disgusting chemical reactions in viewers' brains, viewers who are coaxed and cajoled by the 'evil eye' in the corner of their living rooms to buy things they don't need.

Television sets contain mercury and cadmium, which means they pose a serious eco-risk when dumped in landfills – and the government estimates that 71 million cathode-ray-tube TVs (that's 'old-fashioned TVs' to me and you) will be disposed of in Britain between 2004 and 2010. Why? Because the British populace, so hungry for sensory stimulation at any price, are all moving over to digital televisions and getting shot of their old ones.

When brainwashed consumers peruse new digi-TVs in Currys or Argos, do any of them stop to think of the extremely distressing effect their landfill-dumped old TV sets will have on seagulls and rats, those oppressed creatures who have no choice but to live off our discarded rubbish? Of course they don't. They're too desperate to keep up with the equally mind-raped Joneses next door by getting the latest model so that they can rush home and get their fix of *Celebrity Bollock Swap* or *The Great Global Warming Swindle* or some other poisonous dross that passes for 'entertainment' these days.

As people's outdated TVs fester in landfills, making sick the already oppressed rat community, their new TVs suck up more and more electrical energy. The government says that consumer electronics currently use around 18 terawatt-hours a year, which is equivalent to the annual output of five power stations! You remember power stations, don't you, Esther – like the coal-fired Drax power station in North Yorkshire, which in 2005 produced 20.8 million tonnes of CO_2, more than the amount produced by 103 small un-industrialised nations! Could you sleep at night knowing that at least one reason why Drax continued burning coal and vomiting smog into the sky would be to keep your TV powered so that you can get your fix of 'Trevor McDonald' (whoever he might be)? Did you not hear loud and clear the message of we anti-Drax protesters in August 2006, when we gathered at the power station dressed as clowns and corpses and whatnot, and chanted, 'What do we want?' 'An end to all coal-fired electricity production and a return to a time before there were streetlights, fridges and life-support machines!' 'When do we want it?' 'Now!'

The TV scandal shows just how wild and unwieldy is human-unkind's lust for stuff. There is now an average of 2.4 TVs in each British home! Who needs that many televisions? And what use is 0.4 of a television to anybody? I don't know what the equivalent figures are for America, but given that they are the greediest, fattest, thickest and most oil-addicted nation on earth, I wouldn't be surprised if they had 24 TV sets in each home, five in each room so that they could simply move their eyeballs to watch a different TV channel and not have to exert themselves by pressing a button on the remote control. According to those brave warriors against brainwashing – the Kill Your TV campaign group – the average American child spends an average of 1,680 minutes watching TV every week, but only 38.5 minutes a week having a meaningful conversation with his or her parents! (Actually, that's probably just as well, considering that most 'moms' and dads are dementedly eco-unaware these days.)

As TVs get bigger and 'cleverer', they also get more hungry for electrical energy. The new plasma screen TV uses 390W of electricity a year, compared with the 140W sucked up by traditional CRT TVs. I heard recently that the Japanese have developed a TV with a 103-inch screen! Gaia only knows how much energy will be required to operate such a monstrosity: probably the same amount used by 50-odd small un-industrialised nations. Perhaps all TVs should come not only with a digi-box on top but also an individual coal-fired power station attached to the side, so that they can be directly and instantly injected with the energy created by the abuse of Mother Earth's internal organs.

Of course, the upside of the TV Terror is that it keeps people indoors and fairly static. That is definitely better than having them all walking the streets, dropping litter, binge-drinking in pubs, defecating in alleyways, having knee-trembling encounters in skips that frequently result in pregnancy, and so on. But the TV Terror is washing their minds with irrational consumerist nightmares! We must fight the terror by any means necessary. Step no. 1: DO NOT buy a TV. Step no. 2: tell everyone you know who owns a TV that they are stark staring mad and that they should switch it off, dismantle it and recycle its various parts as something useful, like a veggie smoothie maker, ASAP.

☞ Is it ethical to eat in restaurants?

Dear Ethan,
I enjoy nothing more than a sociable evening spent
eating out with friends. But I do worry about whether
it is right to enjoy eating in luxurious restaurants . . .
think of the expense, the indulgence, the waste, the
underpaid waitresses. One does hear of carbon-neutral
restaurants these days, but there don't seem to be any
in the West End. Help me, Ethan, do you think it is
ethical to eat in restaurants, and if so, which ones?
Gordon Glennon, London

Dear Gordon,
For 'starters' let us take your question in parts (or courses). You ask, is it ethical to eat in restaurants?

But first, ask yourself this: is it ethical to eat? Food is at the very centre of the ethical dilemma of our existence. After all, it is the most obvious way that greedy humans are devouring the planet's resources. We are eating Mother Earth alive, like matricidal cannibals, and turning the marvels of nature into crap (both figuratively and literally speaking). What more appalling symbol could there be of our obese civilisation?

So in a sense, no, it cannot seriously be said to be ethical to eat, in the same way that, if we want to be strictly ethical about it (and some of us do), most of humanity would be better off not existing at all. However, it seems slightly unrealistic to expect the Great Obese – i.e., 'ordinary people' – to accept that inconvenient truth and stop eating, at least in the short term. So in the meantime we need to try to make eating as near-ethical as possible.

It is against this background, Gordon, that we now come to chew over the second part of your question. Is it ethical to eat in restaurants? IN RES-TAUR-ANTS! It is as if you have taken everything that is wrong about the human relationship to nature, cooked it up together into an unpalatable mess, and served it up on a platter in that awful question! People are always asking one another if they know of a good restaurant. But there is no such thing as a 'good' restaurant. Read this carefully, Gordon: Restaurants Are Not Good.

Let us start with the brass tacks, the practicalities of the carbon-bingeing orgy that is a 'lovely' sociable meal out with friends. Think of the food miles – and what about the napkin miles, the cutlery miles, the wine glass miles, the interior designer miles, the muzak miles, the washing-up liquid miles, the waiter's-phoney-smile-miles . . . It has been conservatively estimated by concerned campaigners who researched restaurants around the world that eight of you (I know you always like to hunt in packs) sitting down to eat in a fancy restaurant will produce at least 70 kg of CO_2. This is the equivalent of a flight from London to Paris, or sixty school runs in a 4x4. And, if you can imagine such a thing, it is even less justifiable than those appalling events. Nobody can claim that they need to eat in a restaurant. Ever.

In case you think that I am singling out your fancy foodie friends and their Michelin-starred greed, Gordon, let me assure you that the McDonald's-munching mass of restaurant-goers are, as usual, even worse. I don't just mean that fast food tastes worse (not that the cow-entrail-chompers would notice). We are indebted to the invaluable research done by Stockholm University and the Swiss Federal Institute of Technology, which means we now know the actual truth about the 'cheeseburger footprint' (thank Gaia for those sensible Scandinavians who are willing to invest in the serious work to save the planet!). They estimate that taking everything into account, from the methane produced by the beef and dairy cows to the gas required to cook the ghastly things, every single cheeseburger contains – quite apart from all the appalling fats and chemicals – an average of 4.35 kg of CO_2 equivalent (mmm, tasty!). Now, if you were naive enough to accept the unrealistic assumption made by some – e.g., the people behind *Fast Food Nation* – that Americans eat on average only one burger a week (what, with those thighs?) that would add up to a national total of more than 65 million tonnes of CO_2 equivalent per year. A more realistic estimate of three cheeseburgers per American per week would give a total of almost 200 MILLION TONNES of CO_2 equivalent per year: the equivalent of the output from *20 million SUVs*!

In response to these unpalatable, stomach-turning facts, some businesses have, as you suggest Gordon, tried to present themselves as ethical, carbon-neutral restaurants: they source their food from within a fifty-mile radius and cook their vegetables for shorter periods of time to save on water usage. Big deal! Look, if you really want to set up a carbon-conscious restaurant, try this. Don't source food from within fifty miles; dig it all up from within fifty yards in your back garden, fertilised with the waste from your customers' compost toilet. Don't cook the vegetables at all; serve them on recyclable non-washable leaves, without cutlery. Don't serve anybody unless they can prove that they live close enough to have walked there (demand TWO forms of ID and a bank statement for proof of address), and don't waste energy on lights. There is already apparently a blind restaurant in London, where visually impaired waiters dish up the food in complete darkness. I commend this institution for operating entirely without electrical light fittings and thus showing patrons that it IS possible to live in darkness if you put your mind to it. It is a brilliant example of the Blind leading the Ignorant.

Aspiring eco-restaurants could do worse than follow the Greenhart example. At my dinner parties, eating is a strictly *natural* and sustainable, not-for-fun activity. We endeavour to ensure that no one enjoys themselves. I always insist that our guests do some small eco-tasks between bites: I ask them to spend half an hour on the treadle pump in order to power our non-gas slow oven; or I ask them to empty the contents of the toilet's compost bucket on to our vegetable patch in order to spruce up the stuff they will eat next time they visit. By the end of the evening, as they survey their carefully weighed portions of lentil loaf and rub their backs after carrying out their eco-menial tasks, the guests generally have to admit that they have not enjoyed themselves – and of course they feel better for it.

There is really only one ethical way to eat at a restaurant, Gordon – take a slice of lentil loaf with you when you go to picket the place and tell the customers to stop scoffing the planet into an early grave.

Is it ethical to serve lentil loaf?

Dear Ethan,
I hope you will forgive me for asking a cheeky
question . . . but what is your recipe for lentil loaf?
You mention your love for lentil loaf quite frequently,
and I am keen to cook one next time I am entertaining
friends. But I want to cook it as ethically as possible.
Any advice?

Emilie Rideau, Merseyside

Dear Emilie,

Well, seeing as you ask so nicely . . . ! However, you should know from the outset that a great deal more than lentils goes into one of Ethan's Lentil Loaves. Alongside all the lentils, walnuts, garlic and vinegar, my lentil loaf is also packed full of human energy, Gaiaphilia and the milk of ethically attuned human kindness (but not REAL milk, of course – this is a strictly vegan dish). With such ingredients, my loaf fills the heart with warm and moist feelings of eco-joy, as well as filling the stomach with warm and moist nuts and seeds. Without these ingredients, however, the loaf will end up little more than a nutty, squidgy, disappointing alternative to quiche.

You will need the following:

1 small onion
1 clove of garlic
2 stalks of celery
2 teaspoons of sage
2 egg substitutes
2 tablespoons of wholewheat flour
Lentils (3 cups)
Wild brown rice (3 cups)
Chopped walnuts ($^{1}/_{2}$ cup)
Vinegar (2 tablespoons)
Human excrement (7 buckets)

Step one: Plant your lentil seedlings in some moist (but not WET) soil. Lentils grow best on level or slightly rolling land that drains well. Do not plant them where water gathers and rises, as they will drown and die and you will be guilty of what we in the Greenhart household call a Lentil Lethality.

Step two: Go to the toilet. Pass your excrement through an eco-friendly process of thermophilic decomposition, which will heat it enough to remove or destroy harmful pathogens. You will be left with what is known as 'humanure'. Spread the humanure on the moist soil around the lentil plants to strengthen and enrich it. You will need seven buckets of humanure; do not under any circumstances use plastic buckets. Wait three months.

Step three: Remove the lentil plants from the earth. Note the word 'remove' rather than 'pull' or 'tug': such violent methods of plant-removal would only taint the lentils with the toxins of human aggression and ruin the texture (emotional) of your loaf. The plants should be dug up gently and by hand, and then transported from the patch of land that was their womb into your home by a human chain of hands rather than in any eco-unfriendly device such as a wheelbarrow (can damage soil) or basket (tend to be made from literally weeping willow).

Step four: Break open the pods as gently as possible and remove the lens-shaped seeds – our beloved lentils! This must be done while reciting the Lentil Lament, written by my youngest boy: 'Oh lentil plant, you must think we're mental but we aren't / We only want to feed on your majestic seeds / You shall pass through our derriere and return to the open air.' Put lentils in a non-plastic dish and seal shut.

Step five: Preheat your stone cooking slab to Dark Orange Glow (known as 350 degrees Fahrenheit in the world of gas and electric cooking). If you do not have a stone cooking slab then you cannot make Ethan's Lentil Loaf, I'm afraid.

Step six: Finely chop the onion and celery. Crush the clove of garlic. It should be crushed naturally rather than with a man-made implement: we leave our cloves of garlic on the ground of our chicken coop where they are split and squished by the chicken's free-range walking. Sauté the onion, garlic and celery until the onion is translucent. Add the sage. Then combine ALL the ingredients into a large non-plastic bowl and mix by hand. The mixing MUST be done by the person who contributed most of the human excrement to the upkeep of the lentil plants, so that there is consistency between the rearing and searing processes.

Step seven: Put mix into a loaf pan. Press down GENTLY. Bake in the hollowed-out heart of your stone cooking slab for 18 hours.

Step eight: Cut loaf into slices using taut string rather than a knife. Serve on ethically sourced wooden plates with a glass of self-welled water and an optional dip of Lentil Leaf Sauce (made from lentil leaves crushed by free-range chicken walking mixed with water and naturally cracked black pepper).

Step nine: Go to the toilet. Pass the lentil loaf through your system, and through the process of thermophilic decomposition. Take the resultant humanure to your garden or allotment and spread on to the moist soil around your new lentil plants. Go back to step two and repeat.

 ## Is it ethical to laugh?

Dear Ethan,
I had a really weird experience the other week. I was at a comedy club, watching a female comedian make jokes about her lazy husband and her even lazier ovaries. It was very witty! But then, as I laughed, I suddenly became consumed by guilt. I thought to myself: who am I to laugh when the planet is in such dire straits? Now I'm wondering if it is ethical to laugh at all. Ethan, have I gone utterly bonkers, or is this a legitimate question?
Dack Quinn, Swansea

Dear Dack,
Welcome to the inner circle, my friend!

If you are made uncomfortable by the sound of human laughter, then that means you have reached the highest state of eco-awareness. I arrived at this lofty position seven years ago, when the sound of two women cackling at a bus-stop suddenly made me feel very uncomfortable.

How can they stand there guffawing, plastic carrier bags in hand, while all around them smog is building up and the ozone layer is being ripped to shreds, I thought to myself. Then I knew it, Dack: I had finally fully tuned in to Mother Earth's pain, to such an extent that human laughter came across as mocking her misery.

Dack, it is not 'utterly bonkers' to be horrified by the sound of laughter. Tell me this, is George Monbiot utterly bonkers? Because, like us, he has also risen to the dizzy heights of eco-enlightenment where laughter rings in one's ears like a demented siren. In an article published in 1999 (he has clearly been eco-enlightened for longer than us!), Monbiot complained: 'The world is dying, and people are killing themselves with laughter.' So disturbed was he by the 'gales of laughter' sweeping Britain's streets, homes and workplaces that he was moved to quote Kierkegaard: 'This is the way I think the world will end – with general giggling by all the witty heads, who think it is a joke.'

But Monbiot can see laughter for what it is – a cover-up for our innate soullessness after years of enslavement by the consumer culture. He advised: 'Stand in Liverpool Street station on a Friday evening, while some of Britain's richest people are going home to enjoy the fruits of their labours. Do they look happy? Stress oozes from them like sweat, anger shudders beneath their skin. The drive to make more money than you could possibly need, to buy more goods than you could possibly enjoy, is a species of mental illness.'

Wow – I thought I was the only person who stood in crowded train stations and stared in horror at the commuters scurrying around and giggling! I was pleased to discover that George does it too, and I hope you will take it up as well, Dack. Especially since I am no longer *allowed* to do it. I have been banned for life from going within fifty metres of the train station at Faversham, Kent, after I spent some weeks there telling commuters to stop laughing and asking them if they were aware that they are mentally disordered. Clearly, the train station authorities thought I really was 'utterly bonkers' when in fact I was simply experimenting with my new-found level of eco-awareness.

Today, people are laughing their heads off (not literally, unfortunately) as a way of avoiding dealing with the most serious challenge Gaia has ever faced: global warming. You may be surprised to hear, Dack, that there is a big debate going on about the ethics of laughter. Recently, as Sheba giggled while reading *The Secret Life of a Slummy Mummy* (I'm sure she was laughing just to wind me up), I stern-facedly read *The Pleasure of Fools: Essays in the Ethics of Laughter*. It's a most interesting tome by Jure Gantar, which explores the ins and outs of 'our moral right to laugh'. Gantar, a Canadian academic, makes a distinction between 'ethical laughter' and 'unethical laughter'. He says that 'all laughter can in principle be seen as unethical'. Yes sir, so true! But the most unethical form of laughter, he says, is laughter at something that is 'irreversible' like a physical impairment, a deformity or – yes, you guessed it, Dack – the ceaseless warming of the planet. It is the fact that global warming has become irreversible, an undeniable fact and an unstoppable calamity, that makes human laughter so grotesque today. No wonder it hurts the minds of sensitive souls like Monbiot and me when we hear it.

We're not the first, of course, to recognise laughter as a morally bankrupt pastime. In the past, other small and wise groups of people – some foolishly called them sects – frowned upon the base laughter of the mass of the population. For example, Ephrem the Syrian, an early Christian theologian (306–373 CE), declared: 'The beginning of all destruction of the soul is laughing.' If a hermit or monk laughed, Ephrem said they had reached the 'bottom of evil'. Ephrem prayed: 'O Lord, expel laughter from me, and grant me the crying and lamentation Thou asketh me for.'

Regular readers will know that I am no Christian. Although I admire the pro-recycling bent to eating the body and blood of Christ, I am a staunch critic of the Christian churches' reckless use of unsustainable wood to make crosses and their insistence on burying dead people in the increasingly overcrowded earth instead of recycling them as compost. But let's face it, Dack, there are some striking similarities between people like us, the eco-aware few, and the early Christians. Like us, they were a tiny minority taking on a massive, uncaring regime: where we have to do daily battle against the fossil fuel industry, they clashed with the Roman Empire. And like us, they were gearing people up for the apocalypse: where we are trying to prepare the mass of the population that have fizzy-drink-addled brains and TV-zapped souls for the coming burning of the planet, they preached about the End of Days and the coming judgement of humankind.

So perhaps unsurprisingly, they, like we eco-aware few, also harboured a deep hostility towards laughter – because they knew there was a need to BE SERIOUS and get human-unkind to rethink his unruly ways before the world became a fireball. They especially hated the way that laughter twisted the face. 'Malicious laughter distorts the mouth,' the early Christians believed, where sometimes you could even see the laugher's teeth! Some of those ugly stone gargoyles that lurk in church coves are based on images of laughter. And you know what, Dack? Sometimes I, too, wince when I see individuals throwing their heads back in a fit of hysterics, their teeth and tongue exposed for all the world to see, as they cackle without a care for the planet! 'Gargoyles, indeed,' I think as I walk by them.

Does that make me utterly bonkers? No, it makes me utterly sane. There is simply no room for laughter in a world that is shortly to expire. People are indeed killing themselves with laughter, as Monbiot says – it is their very laughter, which is the distorted manifestation of their ignorance about recycling and organic produce and other burning issues, which will push them towards a fiery death. They won't be laughing then, will they? Actually, they probably will. Silly sods.

What hope is there, Dack? Well, there is always 'fatal hilarity' – death by laughing. Perhaps the epidemic of laughter that is sweeping our warming globe will help to reduce the human population by some small amount through laughter-related cardiac arrests. It can happen. In one recorded incident in Britain in March 1975, a fifty-year-old bricklayer from King's Lynn died laughing while watching an episode of *The Goodies* which featured a Scotsman in a kilt battling a vicious black pudding with his bagpipes. After twenty-five minutes of non-stop laughter, the bricklayer slumped on his sofa and expired from heart failure. His widow wrote to *The Goodies* and thanked them for making her husband's final moments so pleasant. Maybe this is the solution, Dack – actually to *encourage* more fitful and potentially fatal laughter as a possible corrective to overpopulation. Perhaps it is time to bring back *The Goodies*. I can think of no punishment more fitting for those who are selfish enough to own a TV.

CARBON ABACUS

If you have ever taken part in a sporting event, add ten beads. If you have ever watched a sporting event, add twenty beads. If you have ever been involved in a post-sporting event bundle on to the pitch, during which you may have trampled on the grass or dropped some form of litter, add thirty beads.

If you own a TV, add fifty beads. If your TV has a digi-box add a further ten beads. If your TV has more than ninety channels add a further twenty beads. If you have ever left your TV on standby overnight, add 100 beads and DO NOT do it again.

If you have ever eaten in a Michelin-rated restaurant, add ten beads. If you have ever eaten in a fast-food restaurant, add fifty beads. If you eat in a fast-food restaurant more than three times a week, it is highly unlikely you are able to follow these instructions – is someone helping you? If so, tell that helper to add 450 beads.

If you have ever served a meat dish during a dinner party at your home, add twenty beads. If you have ever served a fish dish, add ten beads. If you have ever served a vegetable dish consisting of vegetables grown fifty or more miles from your home, add five beads.

If you have ever laughed, add ten beads. If you have ever laughed at a joke about Al Gore, Zac Goldsmith, George Monbiot, me or the problem of global warming more broadly, add 650 beads.

Note your bead count here:

. . . .

8

ETHICAL DEATH

Someone once said 'death is not the end'. And he was absolutely right. In many ways, death is only the beginning. After death we have the final privilege of being recycled by Mother Nature, whether we like it or not. We do not come to an end, but rather start living a more ethically attuned life as nutrients in the soil and food for insects and birds.

I receive a lot of letters on death. Most people want to know what is the most ethical way to bury their old gran, or whether they should have their pet stuffed or cremated. (Neither! Taxidermy is an insult to animal-kind AND Mother Earth, since it prevents 'your' dog or cat from giving themselves back to the planet in the form of fertiliser. And animal cremation, like human cremation, is bad for the atmosphere. Not AS bad, of course, since animals don't have ridiculous things like fillings and pacemakers, but still.)

Yet other people want to know if it is ethical to cull large numbers of humans! I get the craziest letters asking if, since the planet is vastly overpopulated (true, true), it is ethical to roll out compulsory euthanasia programmes to treat the human plague and give Mother Earth a snowball's chance in Sub-Saharan Africa of surviving!

I always tell these enquirers to calm down. Yes, there MUST be a massive reduction in the human population – I'd say by at least 5.9 or 5.95 billion – but nature will take care of it if we don't. As the deep-green authors, and my eco-heroes, Ted Mosquin and Stan Rowe argued in 2004, reducing human numbers is paramount, and 'this will be accomplished either by intelligent policies or inevitably by plague, famine and warfare'.

So relax, my correspondents, the Great Reduction will come. Just make sure you are ready for it by cannibalising this chapter on how to have a perfectly ethical death.

☞ **Is it ethical to go to war?**

Dear Ethan,
I hope you don't think I am stark raving mad, but I wonder if it is now ethical to support wars, and even to join in one? As a green-living ethical soul, I have always been against war. It is a noisy, bloody and polluting affair, and it often wipes out entire forests and other natural habitats for animals. But I have heard that the weaponry used in war is becoming more ethical, and now does less damage to the environment. Is this true, Ethan? And if so, does that mean we can support wars if we want to?
Natalie Duriant, Battersea, London

Dear Natalie,
I don't think you're mad at all. I mean, what are the two main complaints made by me and other serious, sincere

ethical lifestyle columnists? First, that humankind is destroying the planet with soot and smog and smoke and must stop doing so at once. Second, that this messed-up planet is vastly overpopulated by the human plague (there are at least 5.9 billion too many of us by my calculations).

Now, lo and behold, the armies of the United States and Great Britain have developed new kinds of weaponry that are kind to the environment but which still kill 'the enemy' (i.e., human beings). In a nutshell, or perhaps a bombshell, armies are not destroying the planet as much as they used to, but they ARE helping to reduce overpopulation through the decimation of human communities across the globe. It's a win-win situation so far as Gaia and every right-minded warrior for Gaia is concerned: planet protection and human plague reduction in one fell swoop!

Please don't think I'm a heartless bastard. I have long protested against war. I was a founding member of War Hurts Animals Too! (WHAT!). We attended protests against the wars in Afghanistan and Iraq with placards saying 'George Bush: World's No.1 Animal Abuser' and factsheets detailing the damage done to donkeys by Britain and America's use of cluster bombs in Iraq: many of them have been killed, maimed and traumatised by the war unleashed by Bush and his 'poodle' Tony Blair. (Poodle?! Poodles are actually fun, peaceable and charming beasts, unlike the beast who lurked inside No.10 for ten years. How must all the poodles killed and injured in Iraq and Afghanistan feel when they hear people describing their persecutor and murderer as one of their own?)

I'm also a long-standing campaigner for the erection of a Tomb of the Unknown Glow-Worm. It's a little-known fact that during the trench warfare of the First World War soldiers used glow-worms to read things. They collected together these little critters and used the glow emitted by their bioluminescence (animals, unlike humans, can produce light without producing bin-bags of toxins) to study maps and read letters from home. How many glow-worms were plucked from their earthy homes and slaughtered on the altar of wartime map-reading? How many of them died as they were chucked aside by the soldiers once they'd worked out where they were going? It seems only fitting that we construct a solemn tomb to commemorate their selfless, shining, squidgy sacrifice.

So, Natalie, please be aware that my anti-war credentials are impeccable . . . and yet, as you point out, war IS becoming more ethical and green, and thus everyone who is ethical and green should rethink their attitude towards it. For example, I was delighted to read recently that the Pentagon is pumping millions of dollars into developing environmentally friendly lead-free bullets! Every year, an estimated 17 million rounds of small-arms ammunition are expended on army training ranges in the US, leaving behind more than 150,000kg of lead that can seep into the soil and even infect local water supplies. The new bullet, which will probably be made from a tungsten composite of tin or nylon rather than from lead, will not impregnate the soil with humankind's toxic trigger-happy leadenness, which means soldiers can brush up on their killing skills *without* harming soil or water. I'm sure you'll agree,

Natalie, that this is a magnificent leap forward in the history of human destructiveness.

As the US Army Environmental Center put it, America is devising a bullet 'that can kill you or that you can shoot a target with, and which is not an environmental hazard'. Hallelujah! For so long, WHAT! and other campaign groups speaking for animals and plants that have no voice of their own (or at least not one that we humans have bothered to learn and understand) have wrung our hands over the rape of nature that occurs during times of war – so let us give garlands of praise to Gaia that in the future wars will unfold without nature being raped too badly.

Here in the UK, those mighty makers of weaponry, BAE Systems, are developing armoured vehicles with lower carbon emissions. They are also developing weaponry with fewer volatile organic compounds and other hazardous chemicals in them, safer and more sustainable artillery, and explosives that can be turned into compost once they have been used. That is, once they have already turned the people in an enemy village into compost. This, I think, is the most exciting development of all. Soldiers should be encouraged to clear up after every massacre by collecting together their compost-friendly detonated explosives and the limbs of the people who have been blown up, and transforming them into a 'Peace Peat' that can be used to plant trees and shrubberies where the enemy village once stood.

The Ministry of Defence is taking the greening of war deadly seriously. Its *Sustainable Development and*

Environmental Manual advises that 'eco-design' should be incorporated into all modern weapons manufacturing. 'A concept of green munitions is not a contradiction in terms. Any system, whatever its ultimate use, can be designed to minimise its impact [on the] environment,' said the manual. So true. Just because you are dropping a bomb on a heavily populated area, that does NOT absolve you of the responsibility to 'Think Green'. If we can have eco-friendly cars, eco-friendly coffee and even eco-friendly Tories, then why shouldn't we aspire to have eco-friendly atrocities?

War, what is it good for? Quite a lot, actually. With the dawn of green warfare, we ethical lifestylists finally have the convergence of our two Big Ideas, Natalie: that the planet must be protected at all costs, and that there are far too many humans and some of them have to go. When we say 'Earth First', we should really mean it! And that is why I, for one, will be cheering on the lead-free, carbon-lite, humankind-reducing conflicts of the future – just so long as no donkeys, glow-worms or poodles (canine not Blairite) are injured in the process.

☞ Is it ethical to recycle my granny?

Dear Ethan,
My dear old grandmother has reached eighty, and she says she is now ready to pass on to the Other Side. She has asked me to help in this endeavour by administering a few too many painkillers, and has also requested that I recycle her body as some kind of

fertiliser when she's dead. So many intense requests, Ethan! Is it ethical to fulfil my granny's dying wishes?
Jemima Albemarle, Ulster

Dear Jemima,
OK, my response is necessarily going to be hampered by the fact that it is still against the law to 'kill' your granny – *even* if she asks you to, and *even* if it will be of great benefit to the planet (in terms of reducing the population by 1 and turning the deceased person into grub for grubs, insects and plants). So you will understand if I cannot technically say 'yes' to either of your requests. I can, however, say the following: 'The planet is terribly over-populated. Euthanasia, whether organised by individuals or the state, might be a good way of dealing with this overpopulation. Recycling human carcasses as soil-enriching fertiliser is a wonderfully creative thing to do.'

There. Does that help? I hope so. There are so many winks and nods in those three sentences my head and eyeballs are hurting.

Jemima, let's not beat around the bush here. (I hate that saying! Bushes have rights, too, and should never be beaten.) The planet is really, really overcrowded, and one of the main causes of this overcrowding is the fact that people are living longer. PEOPLE LIKE YOUR GRANDMOTHER. If you don't believe me, just look at the website of the Optimum Population Trust, a very respectable and even quite posh green group that campaigns for population reduction, and which counts Jonathon Porritt – adviser to the government on all matters green – among its patrons. Its homepage says 'TOO MANY PEOPLE' (their capitals, not mine) and it has a World Population Clock which shows the global population rising by two or three people PER SECOND (those *are* my capitals).

In my view, it is high time the government thought seriously about introducing voluntary euthanasia programmes to deal with the crazy over-congestion of the planet by fecund families and ageing couples. The harsh fact, Jemima, is that older people use up more of Gaia's scarce resources than young people do. And if we're serious about judging people and their activities solely by how much CO_2 they produce – which is precisely what brave ethical lifestyle columnists like me have been hollering for – then that means older people are 'worse', more 'polluting', more 'sinful', more 'evil', or however you decide to put it, than younger pup humans. The old have to be ferried around in cars and other motorised vehicles; they require home helps and cleaners who also tend to get about by car or other motorised vehicle; they consume huge amounts of drugs for ailments and chronic conditions, drugs created, lest we forget, through the torture of animals kept in horrific, energy-guzzling, speciesist Guantanamo-style labs.

I propose giving people over the age of sixty the option to partake in a National Exit Strategy, with pay-offs for their families, of course: free healthcare, free university education, mortgage-free hemp-based cottages. But are the authorities interested in my visionary proposal for treating the human plague on the planet? Nope. When I sent a very long outline of my ideas on rice paper to the local health authorities – titled 'Cleansing Gaia of Eco-Unaware Over-60s' – they sent an Elder Abuse Officer to our eco-cottage to enquire after the health of any pensioners! Talk about bad timing . . . we were having a family do, from which Sheba's dad was excluded on account of his continued questioning of aspects of Al Gore's film, which means he was standing in the driving rain and gaping through our kitchen window as we devoured our lentil loaf. I had to explain that this was not 'elder abuse'; it was 'tough love', designed to preserve the Greenhart household from the dirty toxins of denial.

Alas, in the absence of any national eco-euthanasia policies, it is down to you, Jemima, to decide whether to assist your granny in her brave and gallant desire to bring her carbon skidmark to an end, or to allow her to continue living and draining away natural resources while helping to hurtle the globe towards a fiery vortex of doom the like of which neither humanity nor any other beast, including those poor bastards the dinosaurs, has ever witnessed before. It's your choice. As to the second part of your question: yes, if your granny does somehow 'die', then it is entirely ethical – essential, one might say – to recycle her bodily matter as something useful and juicy for parched Grandmother Earth.

Thanks to the monstrosity that is lifespan-expanding modern medicine, we humans spend anywhere between seventy and 100 years doing toxic things to Gaia. So the very least we can do when we die is give her our bodies. There are various ways you can do this, Jemima. If you own a thermophilic toilet, one that converts human waste into nutrient-rich humanure, you might consider depositing your granny's body into it. Some people are bizarrely touchy about the idea of putting a dead relative through the thermophilic process. When Sheba's grandmother Moll died a few years ago, and I asked family members at her wake, in a very respectful and solemn voice, if we could dissect her body and put it in the toilet, I got the sternest and strangest looks. Even my graphic-yet-sensitive explanation of how Moll's limbs, torso, brain and organs would naturally mix with the Greenhart family's faeces to become a form of human fertiliser that is super-energising for the soil and the worms that live in it was met with a stony silence. In the end, Moll was buried in the already overcrowded consecrated graveyard of a local church, in a coffin made from PINE. I wasn't invited; I think the family got wind of the fact (thanks a lot, Sheba!) that I planned to stage a pro-pine protest at the graveside.

If over-sensitive family members deny you the right to turn your gran into fertiliser, Jemima, then bury her body in the earth, in an unmarked area of a wood or a forest, and let Gaia herself – the Great Final Fertiliser of Human Carcasses – turn her into useful bacteria for the continuation of plant and insect life. It is paramount that you do not put her into a coffin, a disgracefully arrogant man-made barrier between our bodily matter and the insects and soil that *need* our nutrients. A coffin is simply further evidence that humankind thinks itself separate from nature, even when buried within it. Instead, remove your grandmother's clothing, jewellery, false teeth, fillings, acrylic fingernails and wig, and lay her in a hole around three to four feet deep . . . I guarantee, Jemima, that you will sleep easily at night thinking of your gran buried in a shallow hole in the forest with maggots and beetles tucking into her flesh and turning her into soil-friendly faecal matter.

 ## Is it ethical to eradicate mosquitoes/malaria?

Dear Ethan,
I would like to help eradicate malaria and wipe out diseased mosquitoes in Africa. And I am delighted that we now have the option of sending mosquito nets to help Africans instead of – yuk, I can barely bring myself to say the word! – DDT. But I wanna check with you first: mosquito nets are ethical, aren't they? I mean, I know they have a bit of insecticide on them, but that's OK, right?

Abel Lynch, West London

Dear Abel,
What a muddled and profoundly unethical letter! Oh my Gaia, where do I begin? ERADICATE malaria? WIPE OUT mosquitoes? Who are we to wipe out anything, Abel? Diseases are Gaia's way of saying, 'I've had enough of human-unkind beating seven shades of Jesus Christ out of me, so here's a shocking debilitating sickness to teach you all a lesson,' and what right do we have to stop her disease-mongering in its tracks? Abel, you are clearly

suffering from the worst disease of all, a mental disorder that sums up everything that is rancid about humankind: *mosquitophobia*.

First things first. I suppose that if someone put me up against a wall and threatened to douse me in oil – or worse, to force-feed me a battery-raised chicken or some other class of supermarket-sold 'food', or to have a conversation with someone called 'Steve' who had just returned from a weekend of drink-fuelled, Ryanair-enabled sex and violence in Warsaw – I would have to admit, through gritted teeth (kept clean with lime juice, not toothpaste), that mosquito nets are 'better' than DDT.

But they are 'better' in the same way that being stabbed in the stomach is 'better' than being stabbed in the heart. Because, Abel, my mosquito-loathing 'friend', whether we throw a net across Africa or spray it with DDT, the result is fundamentally the same: mosquitoes die (the mosquito nets POISON them!); Gaia's defence mechanism is foiled again and humans become even more insanely convinced of the uppity notion that they have the RIGHT to control nature. Do you really want to be guilty of aiding and abetting mosquitocide?

Don't get me wrong. I am a HUGE fan of Rachel Carson and the other early warriors against DDT. Carson's groundbreaking exposé of DDT in her 1962 book *Silent Spring* has saved so many mosquito lives by giving rise to a quite widespread ban on the deadly substance. And, of course, it has had the slightly sad (I guess) but fundamentally Gaia-benefiting side-effect of reducing human numbers by hundreds of thousands, if not millions, by letting disease take its natural, rightful, rampaging course instead of allowing human-unkind arrogantly to stand in its way. If mosquitoes could talk or fashion placards and banners – and how do we know they can't? – I have no doubt we would hear them cheering for their selfless human benefactor and saviour: St Rachel of the Destitute Insect.

The wonderful Ms Carson, in the face of 'expert scientists' who said she was a fool, showed that DDT damages birds' eggs, affects water quality in rivers, and possibly (let's face it, *probably*) poisons humans, too. My good friend Dr Matt Dickson – who received his Doctorate in Insecticide and Genocide Studies from the American Holistic College of Environmental Consciousness, PO Box 1821 – is currently seeking peer review for his own study, 'DDT and The Rise and Rise of Impulsive Disorders'. This will show – again beyond doubt – that DDT, after entering African people's bloodstreams and spreading through migration into Europe and onwards to America, is also responsible for rising mental instability, personality disorders, cancer rates, laryngitis, asthma, road rage, hay-fever, wheat, nut and banana-skin allergies, job losses and rising food, oil and latte prices in both the southern and northern hemispheres. His report will finally blow the argument for DDT out of the water (literally, I hope) by putting the case for a full international ban on this evil insecticide and for the founding of an International Court of Planetary Crimes which would punish those who use, sell or possess DDT with forty to forty-five years' hard labour and a lifetime ban from speaking in any public forum ('public forum' defined as 'a gathering of more than three people at the same time in the same room or outside setting for the purposes of communicating ideas and information among themselves or to passers-by, viewers, or any other sentient member of the human race').

Of course, there are still thousands and thousands, if not millions and billions, of so-called 'expert scientists', Big Oil stooges and other beneficiaries of the capitalist/catastrophist system who actually CHALLENGE Carson's findings, and no doubt they will challenge Dr Dickson's too when he publishes them. These Exxon-backed, Bush-linked, Israeli-armed mosquitophobic mosquitocidaires claim there is no 'proof' that DDT damages egg shells or poisons humans or enters the brain through the bloodstream and causes shopping addiction and other compulsive disorders in people everywhere from Lagos to Luxembourg. PROOF?! What is proof? And what is truth? What is evidence? What is the point? What is 'what' and what is 'is'?

I'll tell you what 'evidence', 'truth' and 'proof' are, Abel: they are elitist, arrogant, man-made categories designed to justify our knowledge-led dictatorship of apparently less intelligent life-forms such as mosquitoes. The fact is, Rachel Carson simply *knew* that DDT harms birds' eggs. Just as Dr Dickson *knows* that it is also linked to increased levels of gout in Germany. Just as I *know* that the planet will become uninhabitable in twenty-eight years and seven months time if we do not reduce our carbon emissions by 92.7 per cent by 23 January 2011. What ever happened to intuition, Abel? Sometimes, surely, feeling is enough to make it right – and I *feel* very deeply that DDT is wrong, evil and murderous whatever those 'expert scientists' might say.

However, there was a big problem with the anti-DDT campaign kick-started by Carson: it implied that the only problem was DDT itself. Thus, the rush was on, almost as soon as Carson's book hit the shelves in 1962, to find an alternative. NO! The problem with mass DDT-spraying in America and Europe in the early twentieth century and in Africa in the late twentieth century (and today, too, in those half-devil, half-disobedient African countries that refuse, point blank, to heed the EU's warnings of trade sanctions and pariah status if they do not break free from their DDT addiction) is that it elevates humankind over mosquito; it tells us that WE own the planet and that WE are 'more equal' than mosquitoes and disease. The mosquito net merely represents a more palatable, trendy, cheap and easy expression of this deeply mosquitophobic twisted untruth.

Abel, do NOT make a donation to the mosquito net campaign. Instead, sign up to my new global network of concerned Carsonists, People for the Ethical Treatment of Mosquitoes, and let us start waging a war in defence of the rights of disease and its winged, selfless incubators NOW!

Is it ethical to be embalmed?

Dear Ethan,
I am ninety-two years old, and I think I will probably die soon. You may think this is good news for the planet, but unfortunately my family want to have me

embalmed. You see, I am an Irish Catholic, and in our tradition we cover the deceased's body with embalming fluids, place him in an open casket, and drink gallons of Guinness as we stand around gawping at his body and talking about the 'ould times'. Ethan, surely it is OK, after all the years I have spent on this earth, to use just a few chemicals after my death in order to fulfil my family's wishes?

Tommy Curran, Galway

Dear Tommy,

Ninety-two years of age, eh? You must be very proud of yourself . . . proud to have spent nearly an ENTIRE CENTURY using up Gaia's resources and taking part in activities that lead to litter and pollution, including, judging by your email, DRINKING. Well done, Tommy, give yourself a pat on the back. (By the way, if your age makes it difficult for you to understand the written word, the previous sentence was laced with sarcasm.)

Is it OK to be embalmed?! You might as well have asked, 'Is it OK for me to wipe out a few thousand insects?', because that is what will happen if your family douses your body in fluids, Tommy.

Now, it is well known that I am not a big fan of democratic politics. Why? Because I happen to believe that a large group of people is a demented organism that cannot think straight, and demented organisms that cannot think straight should NOT be permitted to choose leaders and set the political agenda. However, I do like the

European Union. I get the impression that EU politicians share my concern for the planet and my belief that tough measures will be required to force people to be more eco-friendly. So I was delighted to hear recently that EU regulators are considering banning formaldehyde – the stuff that will probably be spread on you, Tommy – on the grounds that it is a poison that is bad for human health and the environment.

Now, you might very well wonder whose human health could possibly be harmed by formaldehyde, considering that, if it is ever used on humans, they tend to be dead already. That isn't the point. Or at least, it's not the *main* point. The main point is that formaldehyde and other embalming fluids are, as the EU regulators point out, bad for the environment . . . they seep into and poison the soil and, even worse, prevent maggots and beetles and other peckish insects from exercising their democratic right to feast on your flesh when you're dead. What gives humans the right to coat themselves in toxins designed to ward off hungry soil-based sentient life?

Tommy, you need to think about the consequences of being embalmed. If the maggot doesn't eat, then the soil does not get enriched by the maggot; if the soil does not get enriched by the maggot, then the trees don't grow tall and strong; if the trees don't grow tall and strong, then the birds don't have any half-decent places to live; if the birds don't have any half-decent places to live they might die off, which means cats won't have anything to chase after and kill; if cats don't have anything to chase after and kill, they will stay indoors all day getting under their owners' feet; if cats get under their owners' feet, the owners will become ratty and agitated; if cat-owners become ratty and agitated, they will emit Anger Toxins into the atmosphere and might even carry out a crazy criminal act, possibly a mass shooting, as a way of releasing their pent-up, cat-provoked angst.

Do you see what I am getting at, Tommy? If you let your family embalm you, it could lead directly to another Hungerford. Your choice of funeral could lead to other people's funerals – which might be good news for Gaia, but it would be bad news for their families.

People don't seem to understand that no matter how much we try to put ourselves above nature, we're still a part of it. And that is most clear at the time of our deaths, at the final snuffing out of our breath and the arrival of *rigor mortis*. After that moment, we belong fully to nature, to her birds and her bees and her maggots and her beetles, and any attempt to preserve oneself from this fate – by locking oneself in a thick pine coffin or burning oneself to a cinder, through to coating oneself in formaldehyde – is nothing less than an eco-crime. Tommy, you got ninety-two years out of Mother Earth; surely you can now submit yourself to her and fulfil your historic duty as a cog in the ecosystem. Get recycled.

☞ Is it ethical to send a wreath?

Dear Ethan,
Like you, I live close to a council estate, and I have befriended a rather lovely family that lives there.

Unfortunately, the father of the family recently died. Even more unfortunately, I have been invited to his funeral and it sounds like it will be – to put it mildly – a quite garish affair! Apparently he is to be cremated, and I have been instructed to bring a wreath of his favourite flowers – lilies. Ethan, what should I do? On this one, rather sad occasion may I be excused for buying chemically sprayed cut flowers?

Kristin Wakefield-DeCaptulet, Epping

Dear Kristin,

First, please accept my condolences for the loss of your friend. Second, please accept my advice: you must not go anywhere near his funeral! Much less turn up carrying a circular contraption containing pesticide-poisoned lilies! This sounds as if it will be the most unethical funeral imaginable. I mean, I know these people are grief-stricken, and therefore probably not thinking straight. But come on. Cremation?! Wreaths?! There's just no excuse for that kind of thing.

Kristin, if anyone ever required proof that humans are bundles of toxins, that our very bodily matter consists of poisons and pollutants, then all they need to do is visit a crematorium. Here, even in death, we use up vast amounts of energy and cough and splutter various horrible things into the atmosphere. Even the end of all brain activity and the last beat of our hearts is not enough to bring to an end the spread of our carbon skidmark. When we're born, Gaia reels in horror at the sound of the pitter-patter of our tiny carbon footprints, and holds her nose in disgust at the mountain of disposable nappies each of us leaves behind – and when we die, she balks at the explosion of gases unleashed by the destruction of our bodies. From cradle to grave, Kristin, we're like pierced Scud missiles leaking nasty toxins.

The first problem with your late friend's funeral is the fact that he is being cremated. Now I know the family you befriended are probably not in the mood for a conversation about the environmental impact of human funeral arrangements right now, but I really think you should sit them down and tell them in detail just how foul cremation can be. The Federation of British Crematorium Authorities says there were 424,956 cremations in Britain in 2004, and it's gone up since then. Currently, 70 to 75 per cent of all dead people are cremated. Each cremator needs to burn at 760 to 1150°C for seventy-five MINUTES in order to turn man into dust. That means a cremator uses 285 kilowatt hours (kWh) of gas and 15kWh of electricity per cremation – the same amount of domestic energy used by the average single person in Britain in an entire month! What's that all about? Are people trying to squeeze in one more month of single living before they're finally interred in a fancy jar and stuck on a mantelpiece? It's like a final two-finger salute to the planet.

The burning of our bodies also releases horrible elements into the atmosphere. According to the Environment Agency, cremations are responsible for 16 per cent of Britain's mercury pollution, as our dental fillings melt and turn to a metallic/gassy substance. Have you worked out how much mercury pollution your late friend's melting fillings will produce? If not, you need to get on the case! Visit his wife *now*, ask her about her dead hubby's teeth, and then demand to know what she will do to offset the mercury that will be released in his fiery send-off. Grief should never be an excuse for behaving eco-recklessly.

As for bringing a wreath, you simply must refuse: 85 per cent of the cut flowers on sale in Britain are transported from abroad, where pesticides are used to speed their growth. Tell me this, are you comfortable with the idea of buying something that was created with the assistance of chemicals and transported by smog-farting aeroplanes thousands of miles to Britain? More to the point, are you comfortable with going to a funeral at which there will probably be butchered flowers all over the place? I'm not. Once, Sheba asked me to deliver a eulogy at her cousin Will's funeral. At the church there was a veritable killing field of flowers, ripped and tortured and sprayed pink and purple petals everywhere. I made some swift scribbly changes to my speech, and delivered what I considered to be a haunting eulogy to flower-kind, to the 'chrysanthemums and carnations chopped up and laid out on the altar of human folly, as if murdered in revenge for Will's tragic death'. I know I hit a raw nerve with the congregation and the powers-that-be who ran the church, because the vicar cut me short and started babbling on about dust and ashes.

Kristin, people sometimes say to me: 'Well, what is an ethical way to die and disappear?' Of course, the most ethical thing of all is never to have existed in the first place (please bear that in mind, all the wannabe parents reading this). But if you do have the misfortune to exist, then you have a responsibility to live ethically and to die ethically. And the best way to dispose of your body – that two-armed, two-legged energy-sucking, lumbering entity that Gaia has cursed us with as punishment for 150,000 years of human beings playing with fire (both literally and metaphorically) – is by dumping it in the sea.

The instructions for my own death are crystal clear. I have written them in a will on rice paper with soya ink, so that once my wishes are carried out someone can eat the will and reconstitute it as humanure for the beloved lentil plants I will regretfully leave behind. When my glorious moment of non-existence arrives, and there is not even the possibility of my ever emitting carbon or damaging Gaia's fragile surface ever again, I want to be sailed out to an ocean and deposited among the fish and the coral. It is paramount, of course, that the device used to carry me to my final resting place be a handmade coracle constructed from sustainable wood. My body should not be inserted into any kind of coffin, but rather left naked, and shaved of all its bodily hair. It would kill me (all over again!) to think that a tiny fish might choke to its wriggly death after innocently nibbling on my body and getting one of my chest hairs stuck in its gob. There should also be no ceremony or final words at my sea-disposal: I want this to be a clear and straightforward clean-up operation, where the sole aim should be to remove my stain from the planet rather than celebrate my life. Once my shaven, naked, unperfumed body has been handed over to the god Poseidon, to do with me as it wishes, all my worldly goods should be burned in an eco-bonfire. This will involve incinerating my rice-paper books, my hemp-based clothing and non-leather vegan shoes, my hemp-based furniture and my treadle pump-powered laptop, and collecting the CO_2 emitted by the fire in a carbon-trapping device; this device should then be sealed shut, AIR-TIGHT, and dumped in the sea, too. There will be nothing left of me, Kristin. It will be as if I never existed. And because I have always craved non-existence – that most perfectly ethical way of being – I simply cannot wait.

CARBON ABACUS

If you have ever fought in or supported a war that led to the injury of donkeys, glow-worms or other creatures, add fifty beads.

If you have helped to euthanise someone, shame on you – it is against the law. (But secretly subtract 100 beads from your total count for bravely helping to reduce the human population by one.) If you have buried a dead friend or relative in a coffin underground – i.e. rather than recycling them as soil juice – add fifty beads.

If you have allowed a deceased member of your family to be embalmed, add ten beads. If you yourself plan to be embalmed, add thirty beads.

If you have ever sent a wreath to a funeral, add twenty beads. If you made the wreath yourself from home-grown flowers moulded together with tree sap and humanure, take away fifteen of those beads. If you think cremation is an acceptable 'exit strategy' from the planet, and even plan to have your own body burned, add fifty beads.

Note your bead count here:

. . . .

CONCLUSION: WORK OUT THE LENGTH OF YOUR CARBON SKIDMARK!

I hope you have been honestly totting up your carbon abacus bead-count! I also hope that you did not use a lead-based pencil to keep note of your count, since the production of this book has already used up quite enough of nature's resources without readers using lead, too. Now discover how long your carbon skidmark is, and what you need to do to wipe it clean.

 MORE THAN 500 BEADS:

You are shockingly unethical. It is likely that you are a frequent flyer and a Tesco shopper, and possibly even a BOTTLE-FEEDER. It is tempting to say that there is no hope for you (because there probably isn't) but that would be defeatist, and it would only give you a green light to continue living an eco-sinful life rather than at least trying to pull your probably chemical-cotton socks up. Your carbon skidmark is approximately 580 miles per year. Which is disgusting. In order to clean this up, you need to plant an entire small forest of pine trees somewhere in Wales, or construct and erect 418 wind-power windmills. If this is, as I suspect, beyond both your ken and your income, I suggest you stop working, driving, walking and eating anything other than self-grown, humanure-sprinkled vegetables for the next two-and-a-half years, as a way of wiping your slate clean and starting all over again.

 ### 300 TO 500 BEADS:

You are seriously unethical. It is likely that you are an occasional flyer and a regular restaurant diner, and possibly the parent of children who have violin and ballet lessons but you DON'T offset the eco-costs of them. There is some hope for you, however, but you will have to make a serious eco-commitment to reducing your stain on the planet. If you own a petrol-powered motorised vehicle (and I suspect that you do), you must decommission it right away and bury it safely underground. If you have a flushing toilet (and again, I suspect that you do), waste not a moment in arranging for a plumber to dismantle it and take it away. Your carbon skidmark is between 320 and 410 miles per year. In order to clean it up you may either plant twenty trees a year for the next decade of your life, or make a very generous donation to a carbon-offsetting company that promotes primitive forms of farming in the developing world or protects the habitats of gorillas, elephants and other endangered species from marauding humans.

100 TO 300 BEADS:

You're trying to be green – but you're not trying hard enough. It is likely that you use low-energy lightbulbs but never bother to think about forswearing electricity alto-gether and using candles instead. You probably recycle newspapers and glass bottles but it never crosses your mind to recycle your own excrement as humanure or your own urine as energy shakes. You need to up your game. Stop only doing 'green things' that make you feel superior to your noisy, littering next-door neighbour (I'm guessing you live in a terraced house in a mixed-class neighbour-hood – you're at the gentrified end), and instead make some serious life changes that might help change the planet's fortunes, too. Currently your carbon skidmark is between 180 and 275 miles a year – a bit below the national average, but WAY ABOVE what's acceptable. To eco-detergent it out of existence, you must plant twelve trees right away and build a permanent allotment in your garden to grow your own veg. You should use cow manure to begin with, later moving up to humanure when you feel braver.

 FEWER THAN 100 BEADS:

You are on the cusp of being ethical. But who wants to be on the cusp of anything? It is time you took the final leap into the world of Greenhart-style supreme ethical living. It is likely that you live somewhere in the country, perhaps Dorset, and you have a small patch of land where you grow organic veg and keep free-range chickens and a cow or two. You are probably well-educated, articulate and deeply caring, but you lie awake at night wondering if you can REALLY give up modern life completely . . . 'What about cinemas', you think, 'and heated swimming pools?' Don't worry, I thought similar things before I took the eco-oath of non-impact, zero-carbon, insignificant living, and I have zero regrets about devoting myself fully to Gaia. Currently your carbon skidmark is around forty or fifty miles per year – so it's still too long. You can clean it up in one simple step: simply take that decision to turn your back on cinemas and heated swimming pools and the various other mod cons ('con' being the operative word) that you feel attached to, and leap into the ethical void.

 ## NO BEADS:

This section exists only for me, Ethan Greenhart, in case I ever feel like using this book to tot up my bead-count (which will of course be zero) and then looking back here to check out my carbon skidmark. Well done, me, your skidmark is virtually 0.00 miles per year! You are making absolutely no impact on the world whatsoever. And long may it continue.